The Investor's Edge

The Investor's Edge

A Real-World Money Manager Tells You How To Trade Stocks

By Gary Kaltbaum

ISBN 0-9721229-5-8

Printed in the United States of America

Charts and tables contained in this book were reprinted courtesy of Prophet Financial Systems Inc. (www.prophet.net), where indicated.

Disclaimer

It should not be assumed that the methods, techniques, or indicators presented in this book will be profitable or that they will not result in losses. Past results are not necessarily indicative of future results. Examples in this book are for educational purposes only. The author, publishing firm, and any affiliates assume no responsibility for your trading results. This is not a solicitation of any order to buy or sell.

The NFA requires us to state that "HYPOTHETICAL OR SIMULATED PERFORMANCE RESULTS HAVE CERTAIN INHERENT LIMITATIONS. UNLIKE AN ACTUAL PERFORMANCE RECORD, SIMULATED RESULTS DO NOT REPRESENT ACTUAL TRADING. ALSO, SINCE THE TRADES HAVE NOT ACTUALLY BEEN EXECUTED, THE RESULTS MAY HAVE UNDER- OR OVERCOMPENSATED FOR THE IMPACT, IF ANY, OF CERTAIN MARKET FACTORS, SUCH AS LACK OF LIQUIDITY. SIMULATED TRADING PROGRAMS IN GENERAL ARE ALSO SUBJECT TO THE FACT THAT THEY ARE DESIGNED WITH THE BENEFIT OF HINDSIGHT. NO REPRESENTATION IS BEING MADE THAT ANY ACCOUNT WILL OR IS LIKELY TO ACHIEVE PROFITS OR LOSSES SIMILAR TO THOSE SHOWN."

I dedicate this book to my adoring wife Suzanne and my children, Aaron and Eric. The patience they have had while I chart my way into oblivion is above and beyond the call of duty. My wife has been an inspiration since I met her as she has seen many obstacles and never let them get her down.

Contents

ACKNOWLEDGMENTS

I want to acknowledge several people. William O'Neil and Stan Weinstein. Without their teachings of technical analysis, I would be nowhere. Their lessons on discipline, as well as to always listen to the tape, have kept me in good stead.

I also want to acknowledge every human being that ever laughed at me for spending the extra hours looking at the market. Your snickers drove me harder and stronger to figure out what makes the market tick.

I must also acknowledge my parents, Herbert and Thelma, for kicking me in the rear every time I think I am too good at this game. I have learned that whenever I get too full of myself, the market gods come and get me.

INTRODUCTION

In March 2000, most of Wall Street was asleep. Traders and investors had made a lot of money over the previous two decades, during what had been the longest bull market in history. The Nasdaq had been a wealth creator to the tune of hundreds of billions of dollars. People from all walks of life had been making money: Cab drivers and soccer moms carried live quote machines. With calm detachment, as they watched the market plummet, they reassured themselves (aided and abetted by "expert analysts" and the news media) with this mantra:

> **It's only a correction within a bull market.** ***Don't sell!***
>
> **It's only a correction within a bull market.** ***Don't sell!***
>
> **It's only a correction within a bull market.** ***Don't sell!***

By the end of the year 2000, the Nasdaq had lost over 50% of its value. That "friend" who had created billions of dollars in wealth over the course of years had taken it away from millions of average investors, mutual funds and Wall Street institutions . . . in a matter of seven months. Traders and investors who kept their holdings expecting yet another year of double-digit gains, were left with nothing. But there's more. Over the course of the next two years in the midst of many false starts, the market continued to spiral lower. By the middle of 2002, the Nasdaq had lost 70%.

THE ONE GROUP THAT PROFITED DURING THE DEBACLE

Now let me tell you the flipside. There was a small group of people who not only escaped the Wall Street debacle unscathed, but made money as the market declined. I was one of those who clearly saw what the market was saying at the time. Between March and April 2000 and continuing forward as the market headed lower, *my technical indicators and all the price patterns I follow in individual stocks were telling me that the market was going lower.*

> *It is a matter of record that I brought as many people as I could with me. I told my friends. I told the thousands of people among my radio listening audience. And later in 2000 when I joined TradingMarkets.com, I told the thousands of people who read my column. I told them all to get out of the market entirely and even short it, if they knew how.*

THE KEY TO SUCCESSFUL TRADING IS *NOT WHAT YOU THINK!*

Now allow me to let you in on a secret. What you expect me to say may be the opposite of what you want to hear. Be prepared to think and act outside of the box. You see, I am not a genius, nor do I have a formula that allows me to predict what the markets will do tomorrow or next year. But I do have a methodology and an important belief system.

In this book, not only will I teach you how to successfully trade the market, whether it's going up or down, but I will also pound into your head this **new belief system.** That is:

> **Focus on what the market is telling you today. Forget about tomorrow until it actually happens.**
>
> *Trying to predict the markets is the single biggest cause of people losing money in their investing and trading activities.* Sadly, trying to

> anticipate the future is what the vast majority of people want to do, whether they are attempting to invest in order to pay for their child's college tuition or sound intelligent on national TV. Prediction, forecasting . . . whatever you want to call it, is not only futile, it is dangerous!

In March 2000 when I told people to start getting out of the market, I did not predict anything. I didn't go on national TV and say that the market was going into a long bear market. Why? Because frankly, I didn't know. What I *did* know was that my technical indicators and stock patterns were telling me, "This market is in trouble."

And every day since then has been a *brand-new day* in which I read the market anew.

The market continues to talk to me, day after day, week after week, month after month. I just do what the market tells me to do today.

AND NOW I WILL TEACH YOU TO DO THE SAME!

What I have just explained to you is one of the most important keys to my success.

> *You can listen all you want to the market gurus who come on TV making rational-sounding arguments about whether the market is going this way or that in the coming days and weeks. Yeah, it all sounds so good as they use impressive-sounding technical jargon and colorful historical charts. And you listen to them because you hate the uncertainty of tomorrow. But I know (and I hope you know) that these people are seldom right.*

Everything I teach you in this book is designed to help you clearly understand what the market is doing today and only today—not tomorrow. *You will hear me say this many more times, and I do not make any apologies for it. It's that important.*

In the following pages, you will combine this principle of focusing on the present with the tools and procedures I follow every day. By applying them diligently, you can make money whether the market is launching into the stratosphere or an abyss. It took me 20 years and a lot of early painful mistakes followed by affirming success to acquire this knowledge which can now be yours.

Thank you for giving me this time out of your busy life. Now permit me make it worth your while.

Best of luck.

Gary Kaltbaum

PART I

What I Wish I Had Known About the Markets 20 Years Ago

CHAPTER ONE

The Key To Becoming A Successful Trader

You may have heard of the famous advertisement with the headline:

> *"They Laughed When I Sat At The Piano . . . But When I Started To Play . . . "*

Here's my version:

> *"They Laughed When I Analyzed Stock Charts . . . But When I Started To Trade . . . "*

In the early 1990s, I was the stockbroker that everybody in my office mocked and laughed at when I would spend many hours during evenings and weekends looking at and analyzing stock charts.

Today, they are no longer laughing at me. They are coming to me to ask what stocks I am watching and which ones I am looking to trade. I have a nationally syndicated radio show that thousands of people tune in to every day to hear my views on the market and where the action is in individual stocks. I am a featured commentator at TradingMarkets.com alongside an "A-Team" of professional traders and hedge fund managers. I now also appear regularly as a FOX News Channel contributor.

How did all of this come about?

Well, here's my story, along with some important lessons I learned along the way. The beginning may have a familiar ring. I started trading and investing in the early 1980s, not knowing what I was doing. I was pretty much all over the place, reading every stock market book and attending every seminar and following every trading approach.

I pretty much spent 10 years meandering. I had no theme, no discipline. I got by, putting my finger in the air to figure out which way the wind was blowing. But I learned that there is no substitute for hard work, and there are no shortcuts. If you really want to be good at this, you first have to strip away everything you have learned about buy-and-hold, target prices and predictions. You must learn to never lose big.

In the early 1990s, I undertook a systematic study of Wall Street's most successful traders and investors of the past 100 years. I wanted to learn their formulas for success in the stock market. In my studies, I expected to learn a variety of systems with exact rules for buying and selling stocks.

But what I learned shocked me. These individuals did not posses strategies that took me much beyond what I had learned over my initial 10 years. Instead, what I learned from these successful traders were two important disciplines upon which I believe your success in applying what I teach you in the following chapters depends. Indeed, I can safely say that these concepts are the basis for my success as a trader, investor and money manager. *Here goes . . .*

- **Discipline 1:** Know how to manage a stock position so that you will *never lose a significant amount of money.*

- **Discipline 2:** *Don't predict.* Evaluate what is happening RIGHT NOW and act accordingly. I say it now, and I will say it a thousand times: Predicting does not work!

To this very day, the validity of these two principles is continually reinforced, not just in my own experience as I continue to trade and help others become successful, but also in my conversations with traders. Over and over again, they say they operate this way.

If you read the introduction to this book (if not, go back and read it!), then you already know how adamant I am about not trying to predict the market. **But knowing how to protect yourself from catastrophic losses is even more important. More about this later.**

HOW I STOPPED WALKING UP A DOWN ESCALATOR

Besides acquiring the discipline of the best traders of the past century, I also needed a cohesive trading methodology. You can have loads of technical knowledge, but without a systematic approach, you'll just wind up winging it and doing whatever you feel like every day. What's sad is that I not only see the average citizen make this mistake all the time, but also people who manage millions of dollars.

Here's what saved the day for me, however. One day, I read an interview of IBD founder William O'Neil. He was asked, "Has Wall Street lost its way?" He said yes, because people were not taught how to pick stocks and that there was room on Wall Street for money managers and traders who wanted to learn how to make money with strict discipline. I told myself I needed to become one of those people. **Frankly, I saw myself walking up a down escalator, and I needed to get off.**

So I read O'Neil's book, *How To Make Money In Stocks*. Actually, I read it over and over again. And what impacted me and became a part of me was not just the methodology itself, but even more importantly, his philosophy, his systematic method of research and his framework for developing his method CANSLIM, which I greatly respect.

Applying that development framework over the course of two years, I came up with an eclectic approach to trading and investing which used the characteristics of the biggest winning stocks in history to build a checklist that I could follow in order to identify future winning stocks.

I asked the question:

> **What do all stocks that make the most phenomenal gains have in common just before they make their biggest moves?**

As a result, I was able to develop a methodology that, like O'Neil's, combined fundamentals with technicals. But there were also some big differences. (If you're not familiar with O'Neil's teachings, then just skip to the next section. I make the following statements here to clear up any confusion at the outset.)

Differences between my methodology and CANSLIM include:

- **I believe in shorting stocks when they're breaking down.** This allows you to make money when stocks decline.

- **I focus much more on technicals than fundamentals.** In other words, I focus more on the charts and the patterns I see unfolding, how the stock's sector is doing, plus what the market as a whole is doing. Only after I am happy with the company's technical outlook do I look at earnings and revenues as a final filter to ensure that I am not buying garbage.

- **I don't need a stock to be making a 12-month high in order for me to be a buyer.** As long as a stock is putting in a nice long basing pattern and gives me the volume I want on the breakout, it can be well off its highs at the time I enter the trade.

- **I trade both long-term setups and short-term setups, depending on market conditions.** In other words, when you have a runaway bull market, I will try to ride stocks for many months in order to squeeze out double- and triple-digit gains. But in choppy markets in which trends are short-lived, I also have the flexibility to hold my stocks for briefer periods of time.

In addition, there is a potpourri of subtler differences such as the amount of volume I look for in breakouts and breakdowns, my emphasis on sentiment indicators for market timing, and some of the trading patterns I developed which you will see in Chapter 8 on shorting stocks.

WHAT YOU WILL LEARN IN THIS BOOK

Now let me give you a taste of how my discipline works with my methodology. Please don't fret if you get a little lost. I will explain all the steps I go through later. Take a quick look at this chart.

Figure 1-1

Reprinted courtesy of Prophet Financial Systems, Inc.—www.prophet.net

This chart shows you all the price action in Genesis Microchip (GNSS) up until October 10, 2001, just a month after the 9/11 attack. On that date, my **methodology** was telling me that Genesis Microchip (GNSS) was worth watching because it had been building a base for over 12 weeks. Like you probably were too, I was shell-shocked by the events that had occurred less than a month earlier. But I agreed with our President George W. that the best way to give the bad guys the proverbial finger was to conduct business as usual.

So I watched GNSS and many other stocks forming bases every day for several weeks. In accordance with **Discipline #2: "Don't Predict,"** I took one day at a time and did not try to anticipate what would happen. I also maintained an attitude of not engaging in wishful thinking. The attitude of "not caring" enables you to avoid bungling into a stock before all your ducks are lined up and winding up in a bad trade.

Figure 1-2

Reprinted courtesy of Prophet Financial Systems, Inc.—www.prophet.net

On October 19, 2001, my **methodology** flashes a big alert. GNSS breaks out from its 12-week base on monster volume. Investor sentiment was bearish due to the overhanging worries from the 9/11 tragedy. Many market gurus were forecasting new lows were ahead.

It is a picture-perfect setup around the 37 level. **Now Discipline #1:** "Never Lose Big Dollars," goes into effect. A stop-loss should be put in at 33.

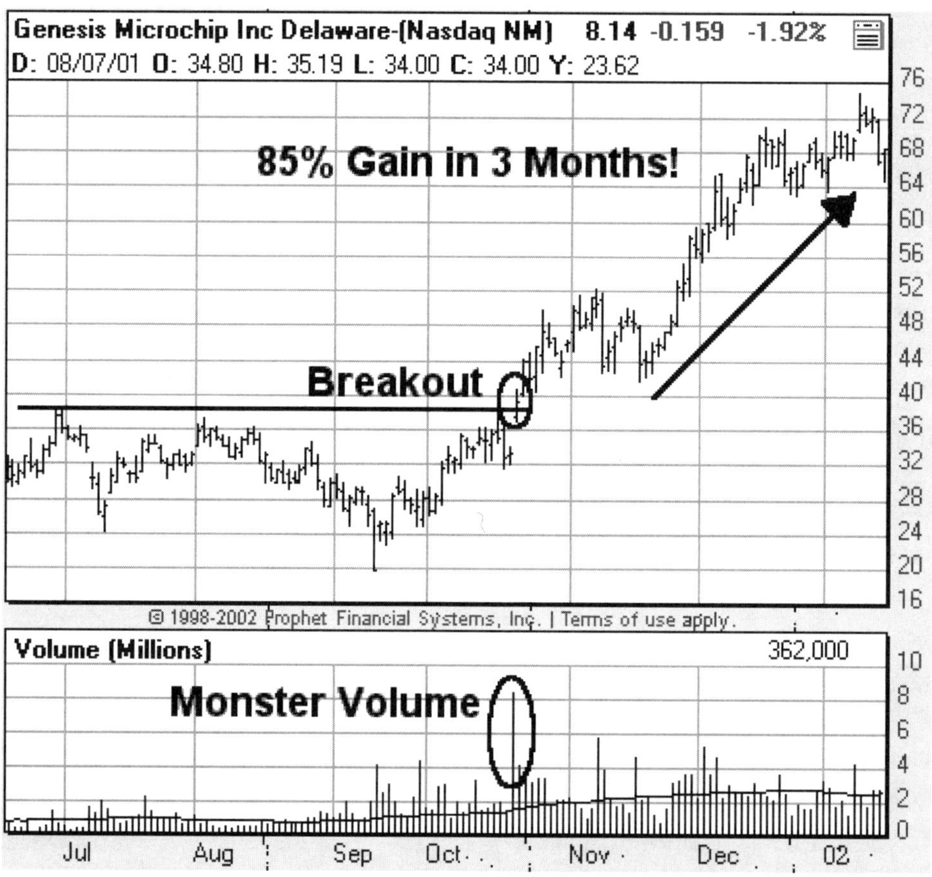

Figure 1-3

Reprinted courtesy of Prophet Financial Systems, Inc.—www.prophet.net

GNSS's breakout follows through and the stock is up 85% over the next three months! In later chapters, I will walk you through the particulars of entering trades like this. But what I really want to illustrate is that:

Methodology + Discipline = Successful Trading.

You probably noticed that I **boldfaced** these words as I worked through my example in the previous pages. That's because it's the same process that the most phenomenally successful traders I've studied have put into practice. It's what I do over and over again.

Most of the trading public focuses exclusively on **methodology**. They search far and wide for some trading system that will act like a money-making machine, telling them exactly what to buy and what to sell. But what everybody tends to ignore, to their peril, is the fact that we are genetically wired to foul ourselves up in the markets. That's why you not only hear about your neighbor who lost a huge pile of money in the markets, but also the professional on Wall Street who manages billions. They all shoot themselves in the foot the same way. So heed my words before you dig into the methodology. The idea here is not only to learn the recipe, but also to put it into practice successfully.

HERE'S WHAT I WILL TEACH YOU, CHAPTER BY CHAPTER

Now let me give you a brief rundown of what I will be covering in this book. If you know something about my background, you know that I am a communicator. I love to teach people how to do what I do for a living in the simplest, clearest terms. I do it every day on my radio show and in my columns. So I promise that I will take you through these chapters as quickly and painlessly as possible without the outpourings of market mumbo jumbo you find in other resources.

I have divided this book into three parts.

Part I: What I Wish I Had Known About The Markets 20 Years Ago

In **Chapter 1**, which you are now reading, I'm giving you the **basic framework** you need in order to execute my trading methodology correctly.

In **Chapter 2,** I will give you the **basic technical knowledge** you need in order to fully understand the rest of the book. And I will teach you how to identify "long bases," the price pattern from which some of the biggest and longest-lasting moves in stocks are launched.

Next, in **Chapter 3,** I will teach you about **breakouts, my bread-and-butter strategy.** Much of my success in picking the correct stocks for buying and shorting, as well as correctly *timing the market,* revolves around this one strategy. In this chapter I will share with you every detail of what breakouts look like and how to recognize them.

Part II: Putting The Odds In Your Favor Before You Buy A Stock

When you get to **Chapter 4,** you and I will get down to business as I show you how to **"time the markets."** That is, how do you determine if the market is going up or down each day? This is very important because the direction of the market determines to a great extent the price movement of individual stocks. You will have a great edge when you only buy or sell stocks in sync with the overall market.

In **Chapter 5,** I will teach you how to use **industry group analysis** to boost the odds of winning whenever you buy or short a stock, regardless of whether the market is headed higher or lower.

> From here, we will put together all the pieces of knowledge that you've learned in Chapters 2 through 5, so that . . .

. . . in **Chapter 6,** you will learn how to consistently select stocks that could possibly achieve maximum gains. I will show you how to hunt down the right candidates by combining breakout patterns with market timing, industry group analysis, and the other important analysis tools I use.

Part III: Trading Stocks The Gary Kaltbaum Way

In **Chapter 7,** I will walk you through real world examples of how to systematically apply my approach to **buying individual stocks.** You will learn the patterns, price and volume relationships, and market conditions that, working together, tell me that a stock is ready to be bought.

In **Chapter 8,** I will show you, through more real world examples, how to make money when stocks go down, by **selling short.** During the worst phase of a bear market, virtually everything plummets. So this is knowledge you should know how to apply.

Finally, in **Chapter 9,** I will provide you with a **solid foundation** for taking all of the knowledge in this book and applying it correctly. I will give you an inside look at how I spend my nights and weekends doing the research necessary in order to be ready every morning with my buy and sell candidates. And I will also provide you with my *10 Essential Rules For Stock Market Success.*

Let's get started!

CHAPTER TWO

How To Read A Chart Like A Professional Trader

This chapter is intended for people unfamiliar with stock charts and basic technical analysis. If you already know what a stock chart is and what terms like "open," "high," "low" and "close" mean, then you can probably skip this chapter and move on to the next. However, if this is unfamiliar territory, I suggest you spend some time with me now as I teach you the basics.

Legendary money manager Warren Buffett once said:

> In the business world, the rearview mirror is always clearer than the windshield.

I agree with Mr. Buffett wholeheartedly. That is why I strive to remain uncommitted to any particular opinion about what might happen in the future. But on the other hand, to be completely unbiased is impractical. I would not be able to make any decisions about where to invest money unless I was able to have an opinion about which stocks looked most attractive.

The point I'm making is that you have to be flexible and willing to admit tomorrow that the view you held today was wrong and then reevaluate on the basis of new information that flows to you every day.

OK, so the question now is how do you form the best possible opinion about what stocks to buy? Most of what you need to know is to be found in the many decades of historical price-and-volume action that you can actually see just by looking at widely available stock charts. In this chapter I will give the basic foundation of knowledge that you need to look at a chart and quickly spot potential investment and trading opportunities.

Having said that, let me also tell you the worst possible way to form your opinion about which stocks to buy.

You won't find the answers in the opinions of stock analysts and financial gurus you see on TV, radio or newspaper or the fellow you meet at the train station. And, in fact, I'm telling you that you don't even need to listen to yours truly in order to arrive at a solid decision about which stocks you should be focusing on. I sincerely want to help you to be self-sufficient and determine your very own destiny, rather depending on others.

WHAT IS A STOCK CHART?

A stock chart is a visual representation of the daily price fluctuations of stocks through history. Each day, supply and demand pressures stemming from the activities of buyers and sellers drive the price of stocks either up or down or even sideways. By the end of the day when trading is over, the price settles at what is called the "close." The close, together with other bits important information, is plotted day by day on a chart so that you can see price trends as they develop. There are different time frames that you can look at. In this book we will mainly be focusing on two types of charts

1. Charts that show the closes for *each day*, also known as daily charts

2. Charts that show the closes for *each week*, also known as weekly charts

There are other varieties such as 5-minute charts used by daytraders, and quarterly and yearly that are used by long-term investors. We won't concern ourselves with these.

HOW CAN A STOCK CHART HELP YOU FIND THE BEST STOCKS TO BUY?

What makes charts such a vital tool for me is that during the course of history there are patterns that repeat themselves over and over again. These patterns can tell you that a stock has the potential to make a strong move. Once I teach them to you, they should be easily recognizable. They form the basis for how I operate as an investor and trader.

In this chapter I will teach you the basics of what you need to know to understand the visual information that is embedded in stock charts and then I will show you how to recognize my favorite chart patterns.

Let's break a bar chart down into its main components.

There are two main pieces of information that I pay attention to on a daily basis for the major stock indices and individual stocks that I am monitoring. They are price and volume.

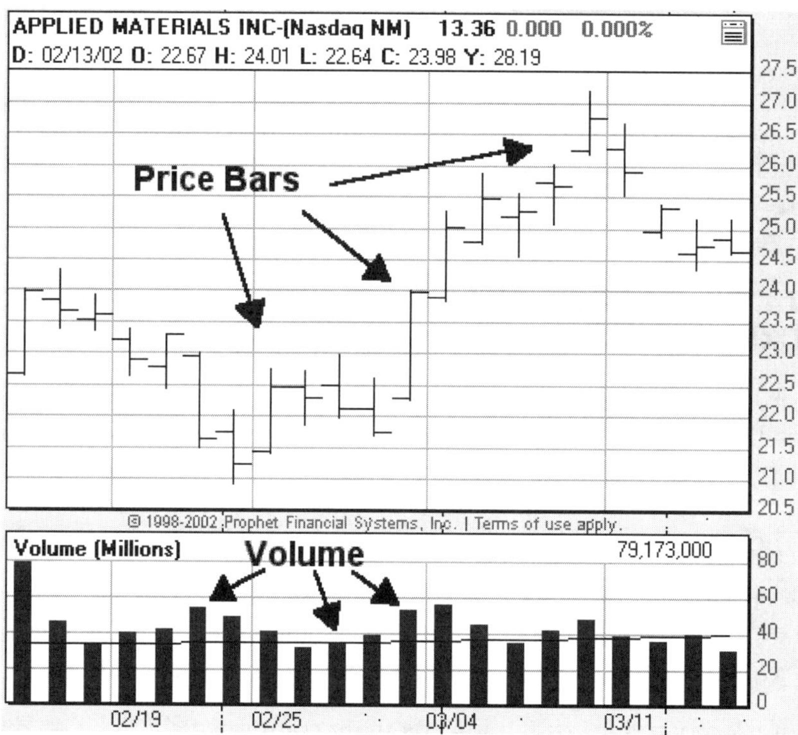

Figure 2-1 Reprinted courtesy of Prophet Financial Systems, Inc.—www.prophet.net

Each price bar on the chart represents a day's worth of price action. Each volume bar represents the number of shares that were traded for a single day.

If we zoom up close and look at price and volume information for each individual day, you will see some more detailed information.

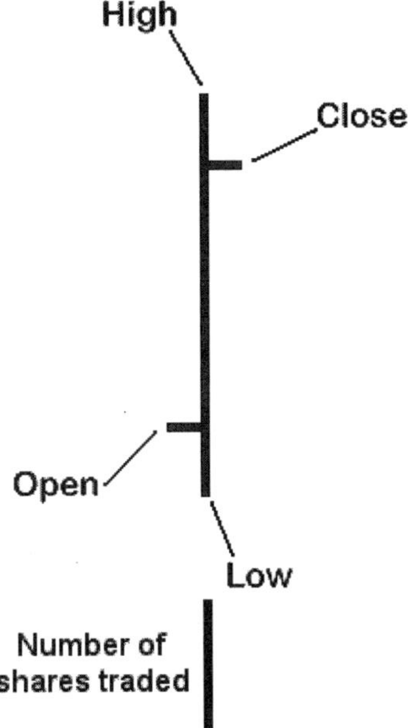

Figure 2-2

- High: That highest price that a security traded at for that day.
- Close: The price a security settled at the end of the trading day.
- Open: The price a security opened at the beginning of the trading day.
- Low: The lowest price that a security traded at for that day.

  And the *volume bar* below the price bar represents the number of shares that were traded for that day. The higher the bar, the more shares were traded. The lower it is, the fewer shares were traded.

Another term that I use all the time is "Trading Range," which refers to the trading that occurred between the high and low during the trading day as well as over many weeks. A small trading range often tells you that the market is undecided. A large trading range often means that a market is making a decisive move in one direction or another.

At end of a day's trading session, the closing price and volume are used to update charts. Over time, you can see some very interesting patterns develop.

PATTERNS THAT PRECEDE OPPORTUNITIES

The most reliable patterns that I know of, after researching stock charts going back many decades, are based upon the following premise:

> A stock will often move sideways for a long period of time before it makes a strong move higher (or lower).

Many of the greatest, most powerful gains in individual stocks were preceded by long, boring periods of sideways movement. Stocks that exhibit this type of uneventful behavior are often passed over and ignored by investors. But, history shows over and over again that these can be the very stocks that make the largest gains as long as certain criteria are met. I will teach you these criteria in Chapter 6.

For now, let's focus on these quiet sideways patterns that can tip you off to what may be tomorrow's winning stocks.

There are important concepts to understand at this point: "support" and "resistance." Here are my definitions:

Support

> A price level many traders view as a bargain price at which to buy. You can find strong support on a chart by looking for price levels at which price tends to consistently bounce *up* from over the course of at least several days to several months. The longer the period of time the support level endures, the stronger it is deemed to be.

Resistance

> A price level which, when researched, tends to trigger selling among many traders. You can find strong resistance by looking for levels at which price tends to consistently bounce *down* from over the course of at least several days to several months. The longer the period of time the resistance level endures, the stronger it is deemed to be.

If strong support and resistance levels are established and the price action of a stock bounces between these levels for a long period of time, then the resulting sideways price behavior is called a "base." It is the base from which the best moves in a stock often occur. The longer and flatter the base, the better. So we look for long bases with narrow ranges to develop. Here is a more formal definition of "long base."

Long Base

> A long base is a pattern in which the price action of a stock moves narrowly between a support and resistance level for a period of 8 weeks or longer.

Long bases are one of the key patterns I look for. Every day and every week, I flip through thousands of charts in search of these bases. The beauty of this is that they are relatively easy to recognize.

Let me show you a few examples and you'll see what I mean:

Figure 2-3 Reprinted courtesy of Prophet Financial Systems, Inc.—www.prophet.net

In this example, of GMST, you can see clear resistance at A, C and E. The support is at B, D and F.

The price action just bounces between these two levels for well over the required minimum of 8 weeks. Eventually it breaks above that resistance level. I will explain how I go about buying a stock at the time of the breakout in Chapter 6.

Here's another example of this easily recognizable pattern:

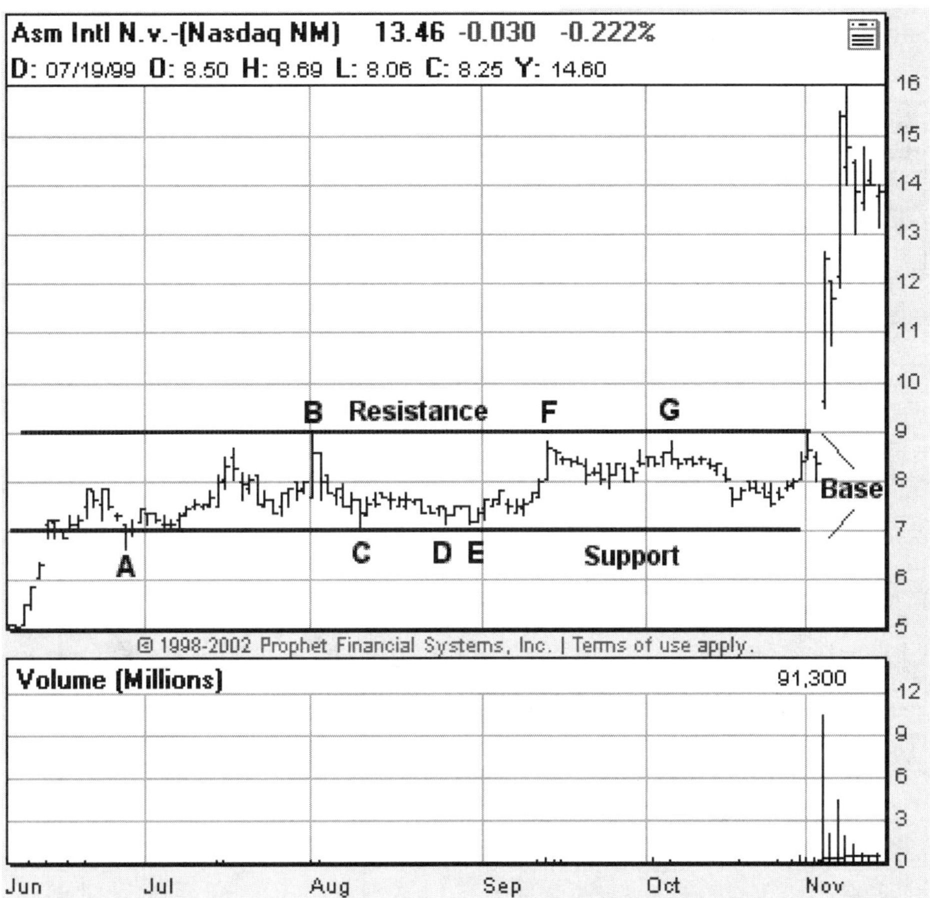

Figure 2-4 Reprinted courtesy of Prophet Financial Systems, Inc.—www.prophet.net

ASMI finds support for 5 months at A, C, D and E and the resistance shows up at B, F, and G. Eventually, the stock breaks out above the resistance and goes straight up from there.

Now do you see why this pattern is so interesting to me?

Same thing for Biovail (BVF):

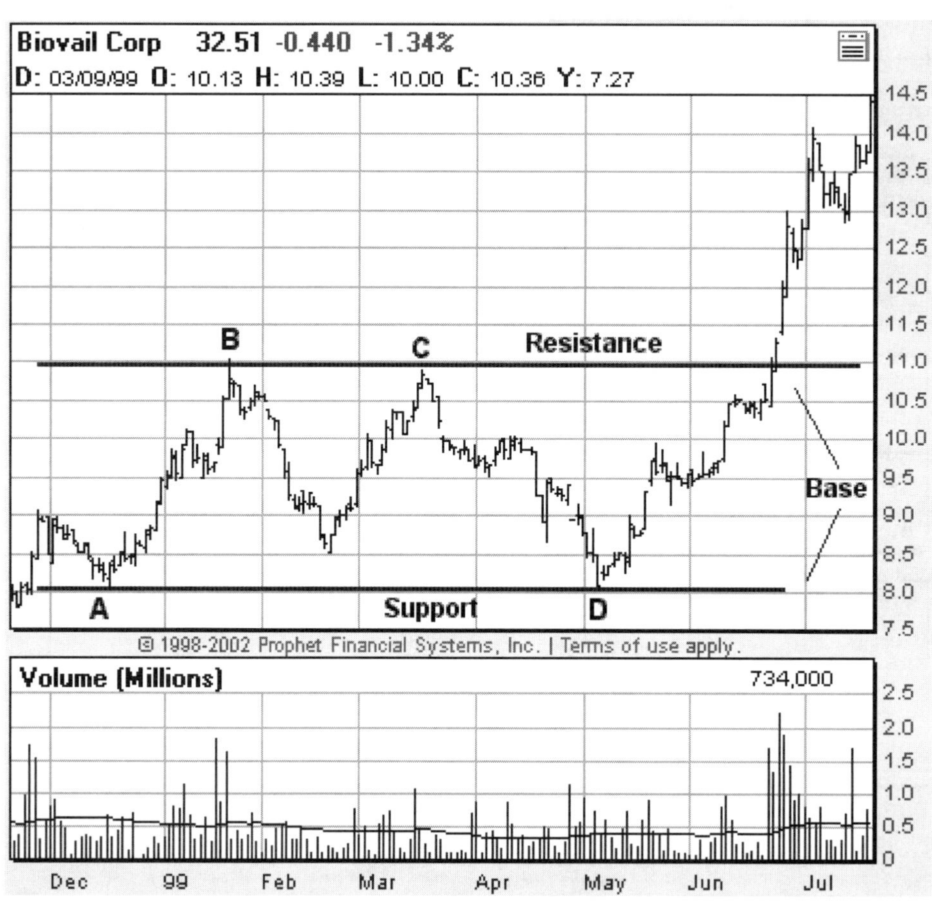

Figure 2-5 Reprinted courtesy of Prophet Financial Systems, Inc.—www.prophet.net

Support is at A and D. Resistance is at B and C. After 7 months, the stock blasts above the resistance level.

WHAT IS THE CUP WITH HANDLE PATTERN AND WHY IS IT IMPORTANT?

Now that you have some familiarity with my bread-and-butter pattern, long bases, let me show you one very important variation on that pattern: the "cup with handle."

A cup with handle has some similarities with the long base in that the price action is contained between a support and resistance level. Many people get confused because they want the cup with handle pattern to conform to a particular shape that actually resembles a real cup and handle. But, in my experience, there are many legitimate cup with handle patterns that look nothing like what you sip coffee from.

Let me simplify things for you a bit by giving you my own description of a cup with handle pattern:

> A cup with handle is a pattern in which the price action of a stock moves narrowly between a support and resistance level for a period of 8 weeks or longer. But the difference between this and a long base is that the price action of a cup with handle stays close to the support level for an extended period of time.

Instead of bouncing like a ping-pong ball between support and resistance, the price action rolls along the support levels for a long period of time before climbing upwards to revisit the resistance levels.

Here is a visual depiction of what you typically see in a cup with handle:

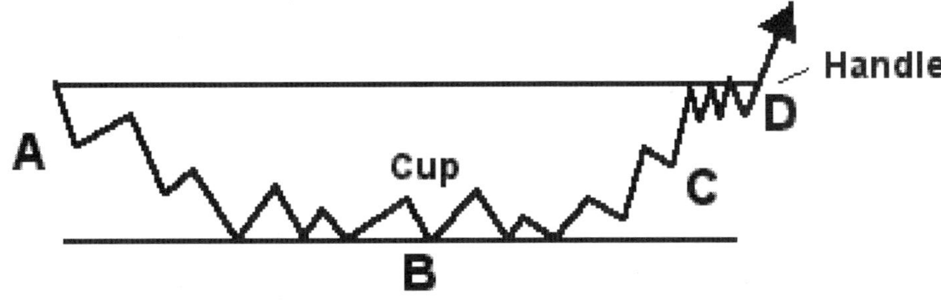

A. The price action drifts down from resistance level.

B. Upon reaching support, the price moves for a period of time along that support level.

C. It creeps higher back toward the resistance level.

D. When it reaches the resistance level, it forms a narrow trading range for a few days and then makes a strong breakout above the resistance level.

You can see how one might see a resemblance between this pattern and its real-live counterpart. But it's best not to be too legalistic about it.

SOME TIPS FOR FINDING CUP WITH HANDLES

Cup with handles are not quite as straightforward as long bases, so let me give you a few extra tips that will help you find them. Later in this book you'll gain some practice that will help you to quickly recognize them through many real life examples.

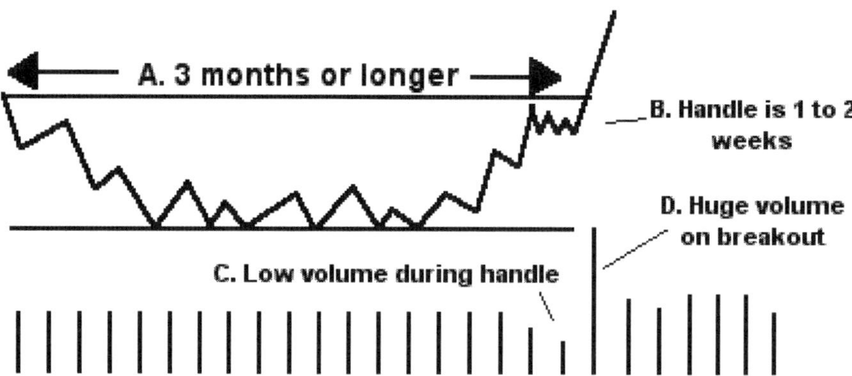

A. Look for the whole pattern to last 3 months or longer.

B. Usually before the breakout, there is a tightening of the price action which is called a "handle." The handle usually lasts one to two weeks. But that is not a hard-and-fast rule. You can get a feel for the handle length by going through the real world examples later in this book.

C. I prefer to the see a handle that drifts sideways or lower on weak volume. That sort of action usually washes the weak hands out of a stock, just prior to a strong move higher.

D. When the stock breaks above the resistance level, it should do so on heavy volume. For large-cap stocks, I like to see at least 1.5 times the average daily volume (averaged over the most recent 30 days). If the stock is a small- to mid-cap stock, at least 2 to 3 times the average daily volume will work.

WANT REALITY? STICK WITH THE CHARTS!

When you trade, a lot of information is bombarding you from all sides. And if you are like most traders and investors, your natural impulse will be to soak in as much of it as possible, in the hopes of finding that one magical piece of information that can help you find the next Microsoft or Wal-Mart.

There is a powerful allure to stocks that have a good story and analysts and TV commentators are good at telling stories. But it is often the case that by the time you hear these stories, the stock may already have been climbing for several months and may be on the verge of collapsing as investors who are late to the game try to climb aboard the train.

My suggestion is to do the opposite of what the public does and focus mainly on what stock charts have to tell you. In my many years of experience studying the markets, nothing gives me a more accurate reflection of reality than a chart.

You see, potential winners aren't yet obvious to the general public and the financial journalists. They are the proverbial diamonds in the rough that are barely noticed no-name companies. They are just trading along sideways as major Wall Street institutions track their earnings growth and stealthily accumulate shares.

Charts are your main tools for finding them.

SUMMARY OF WHAT I LOOK FOR IN A CHART

Look for a long narrow base to form. The longer and narrower it is, the higher the probability that a breakout will be followed by a long, extended move.

Here are the general characteristics to look for:

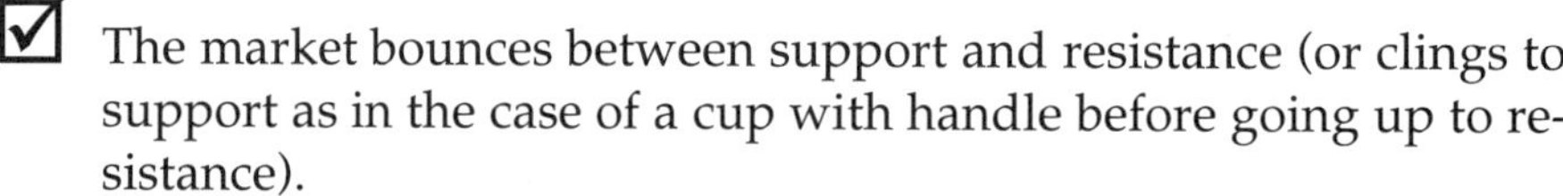

- ☑ The market bounces between support and resistance (or clings to support as in the case of a cup with handle before going up to resistance).
- ☑ It does this for 8 weeks or more.

Once a base has formed, then I'll be looking for a breakout. A good breakout has the potential to give you a move that can last for several days to several months. The window of opportunity for entering a breakout is short-lived, but in the coming chapters, I will teach how to quickly recognize breakouts that are worth buying . . . *before the move becomes obvious to the rest of the world.*

CHAPTER THREE

Here's The Pattern I Make My Living From

If I was stuck on a desert island with only one pattern to use for trading and investing, it would be breakouts!

In this chapter, I will teach you all about **breakouts**, a chart pattern that is at the core of my trading and which plays a major role in virtually every aspect of the market analysis I do.

- When I teach you about market timing, **breakouts** play an integral role in helping me identify major market turns.
- When I walk you through my stock selection process each night as I prepare for the next day of trading, it is **breakouts** I am searching for in stocks and sectors.
- When I monitor the price action during the trading day looking for stocks to buy or short, **breakouts** are what I am targeting, just as a shark seeks its prey.

- As I look to control my risk in all my trades by placing stops, it is how the price action following **breakouts** unfolds that determines whether I have a winner or whether I take a small loss and move on to the next trade.

So much of what I teach you in the coming chapters revolves around breakouts that I believe that teaching it to you early in this book will make everything that follows crystal clear. In fact, you'll already see how breakouts tie in with Market Timing in the very next chapter.

WHAT IS A BREAKOUT?

To help you understand what breakouts are, I start by pointing out the obvious. I realize you already know this, but you'll see in a moment how these simple observations lead to something very powerful.

There are three basic things that the market can do. It can:

- Go up
- Go down
- Go sideways

Each day I look at what the market is doing in order to determine which of these states the market is in.

Now I have a point of reference that is rather unique in this business. Most traders and market technicians follow one of two possible themes:

- **Some focus on trends**. When they observe the market going up, they say that the market is in an uptrend and is likely to head higher. At various key strategic points, such as when the market pauses or pulls back a little, they'll try to buy into it on the assumption that the uptrend will resume.
- **Others focus on predicting market bottoms and tops.** For the most part, the crowd that does this is wrong the vast majority of

the time. I honestly don't know what motivates them, other than the fact that it generates a lot of publicity.

I see things differently.

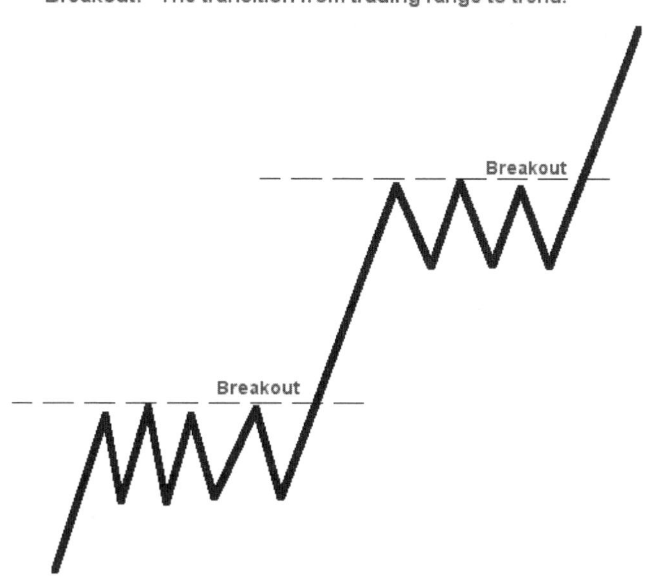

Figure 3-1

My point of reference is the transitional phase from a sideways market to a trending market. When I make a determination about what today's market is doing, I always view it in the context of where it is in terms of that "sideways to trending" transitional phase. *In other words, I am always trying to figure out: Are we beginning that transition today? Or are we in a trend that came about after the transition? Are we at the tail end of a trend and going back to a sideways condition?*

The term that I use every day and in the rest of this book to describe this transition from a sideways to trending market is **"breakout."**

HOW TO RECOGNIZE A BREAKOUT SETUP THAT CAN POTENTIALLY LEAD TO A SUBSTANTIAL MOVE

Now, I will combine the basics that I taught you in the previous chapter with the concept of breakouts and show you how they fit together to become my most powerful trading strategy.

Look closely at this diagram. It shows you all the technical ingredients that must come together to form a potentially explosive breakout setup.

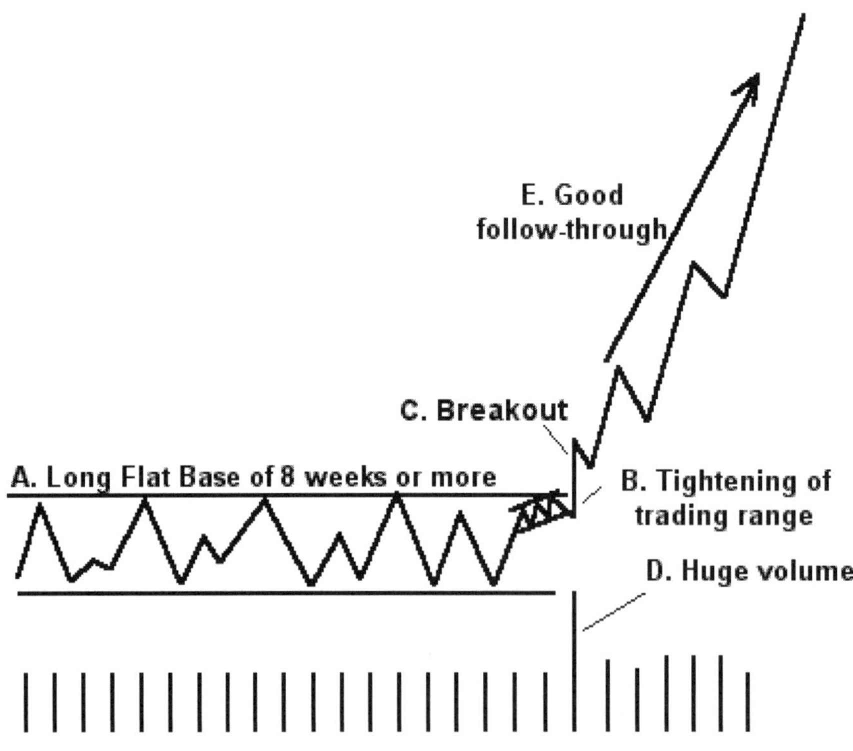

Figure 3-2

To find the breakouts that produce the best trading opportunities, here's what you do:

☑ **A: Identify a base of 8 weeks or more in duration as taught in the previous chapter.** The ideal characteristics include the following:

- **The longer the base, the better.** In my experience, bases that are substantially longer than two months in duration tend to produce the most powerful and longest lasting moves.

- **The flatter the base, the better.** Flat bases tend to produce fast and immediate huge gains at the beginning of a move. I have seen stocks explode out of a flat base and double in a single month. How do I define a flat base? This is a little subjective, but you also will want to favor bases in which the range between the support and resistance level is relatively small. For example, if you find a base that is trading between 45 and 50, you should be watching it like a hawk. If, on the other hand, it is trading between 25 and 50, it's not as interesting.

☑ **B: Look for a short-term tightening of the trading range to occur over the course of 3 to 7 days whenever the price action rallies to resistance.** This is the clue that tells you that a breakout may be about to happen. This short-term congestion isn't mandatory, but when you see this little pattern, you should immediately shift to high-alert status.

☑ **C: Watch for one day on which the price breaks above the base's resistance level.**

☑ **D: Make sure there is huge volume accompanying the breakout.** For small- to mid-cap stocks I need to see 2 to 3 times the average daily volume (averaged over the past 30 days). For bigger-cap stocks, 1.5 times the average daily volume will do the trick. The heavy volume indicates that institutions are heavily buying into the stock. That provides fuel for a long, extended rise.

☑ **E: Look for the price action that begins on the breakout day to be fast, explosive, and long-lasting.** This is why I like breakouts so much. When all the pieces line up together with other supportive criteria I will teach you in Chapter 6, they tend to produce immediate substantial gains. If, on the other hand, the breakout peters out within a few days, then something is wrong. I get out immediately. I don't even wait for my stop-loss to get hit (discussed in Chapter 9).

Here is a variation on the breakout setup before we move on. All of the steps are the same, except instead of a long flat base, we are looking for **a cup with handle pattern.**

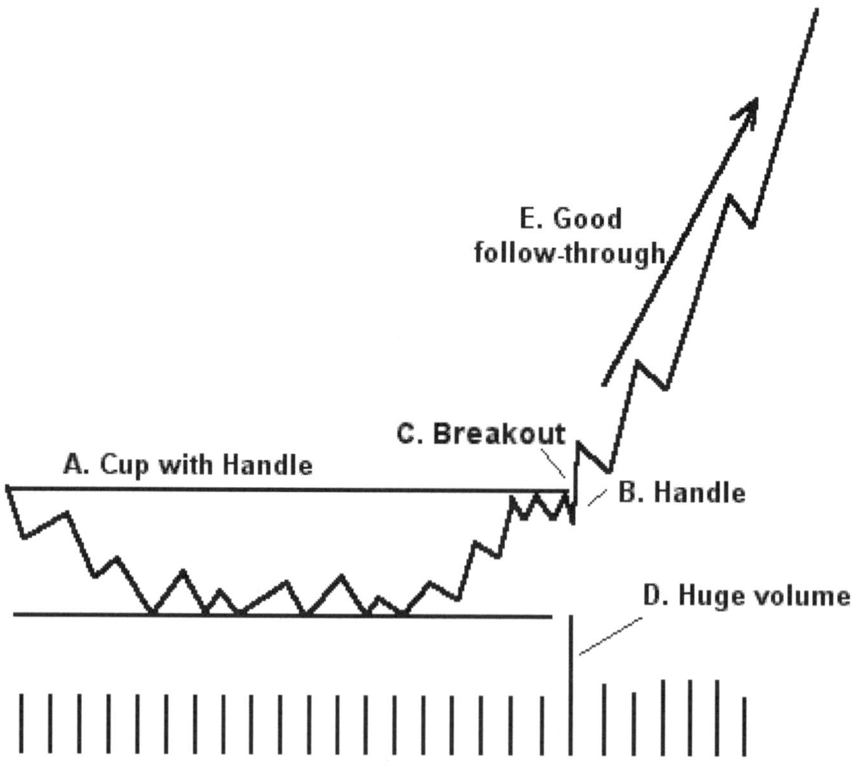

Figure 3-3

To find the cup with handle (see Chapter 2) that produces the best trading opportunities, here's what you do:

- ☑ **A: Identify a cup with handle pattern of 8 weeks or more.** This is a subjective pattern which is best described through real examples. You'll find those in Chapter 7.
- ☑ **B: Look for the "handle," which is a short-term tightening of the trading range over the course of 3 to 7 days, forming on the right side of the pattern.** This is the clue that tells you that a breakout may be about to happen. When you see this handle, you should immediately shift to high-alert status.
- ☑ **C: Watch for one day on which the price breaks above the handle.**
- ☑ **D: Make sure there is huge volume accompanying the breakout.** For small- to mid-cap stocks, I need to see 2 to 3 times the average daily volume (averaged over the past 30 days). For bigger-cap stocks, 1.5 times the average daily volume will do the trick.
- ☑ **E: Look for the price action that begins on the breakout day to be fast, explosive, and long-lasting.** As with breakouts from long flat bases, if the up-move peters out within a few days, then something is wrong. I get out immediately. I don't even wait for my stop-loss to get hit (discussed in Chapter 9).

Now let me walk you through some examples and show you how to put these steps into action. *Keep in mind that while breakouts are the core of my methodology, there are still some essential elements beyond the chart itself that are needed to produce the best results. I will show you this in the following chapters.*

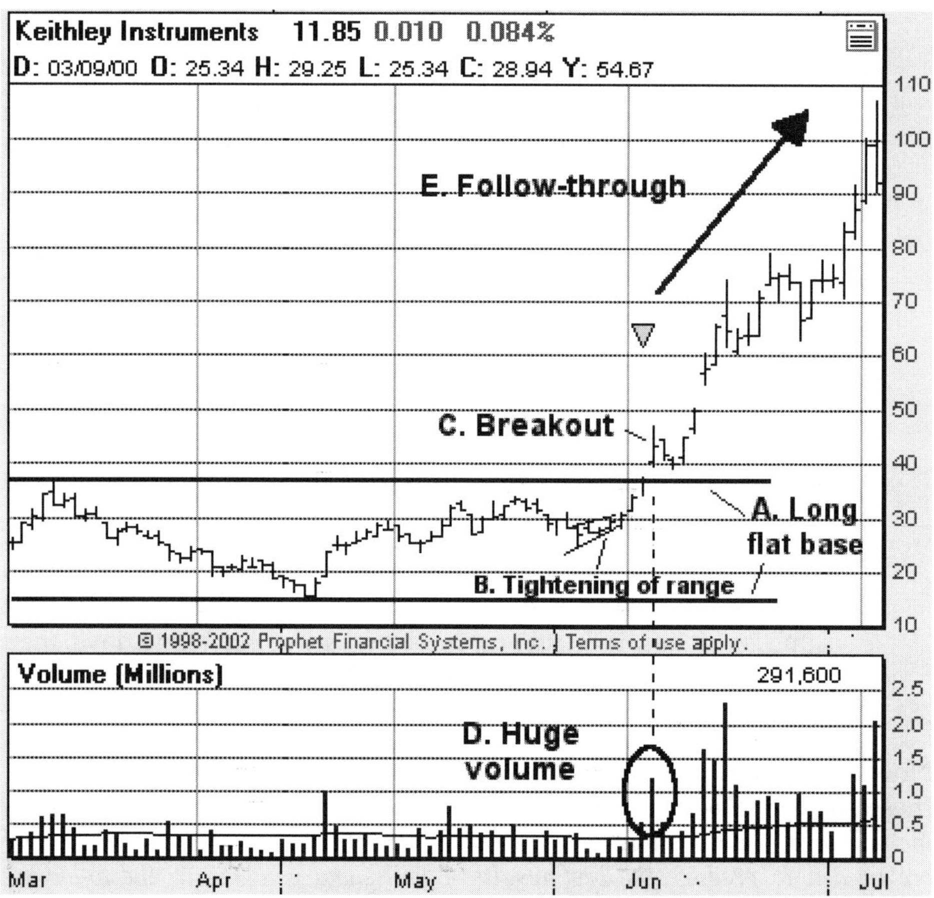

Figure 3-4

Reprinted courtesy of Prophet Financial Systems, Inc.—www.prophet.net

Let's walk through the steps in this chart of Keithley (KEI):

- ☑ A: Long flat base of 3 months, more than our minimum of 8 weeks.
- ☑ B: A brief tightening of the price action as it approaches the top of the base.
- ☑ C: Price breaks out above the base.
- ☑ D. Huge volume.
- ☑ E: Relentless follow-through with only minor pauses.

After this textbook breakout, Keithley was up over 100% in just a month.

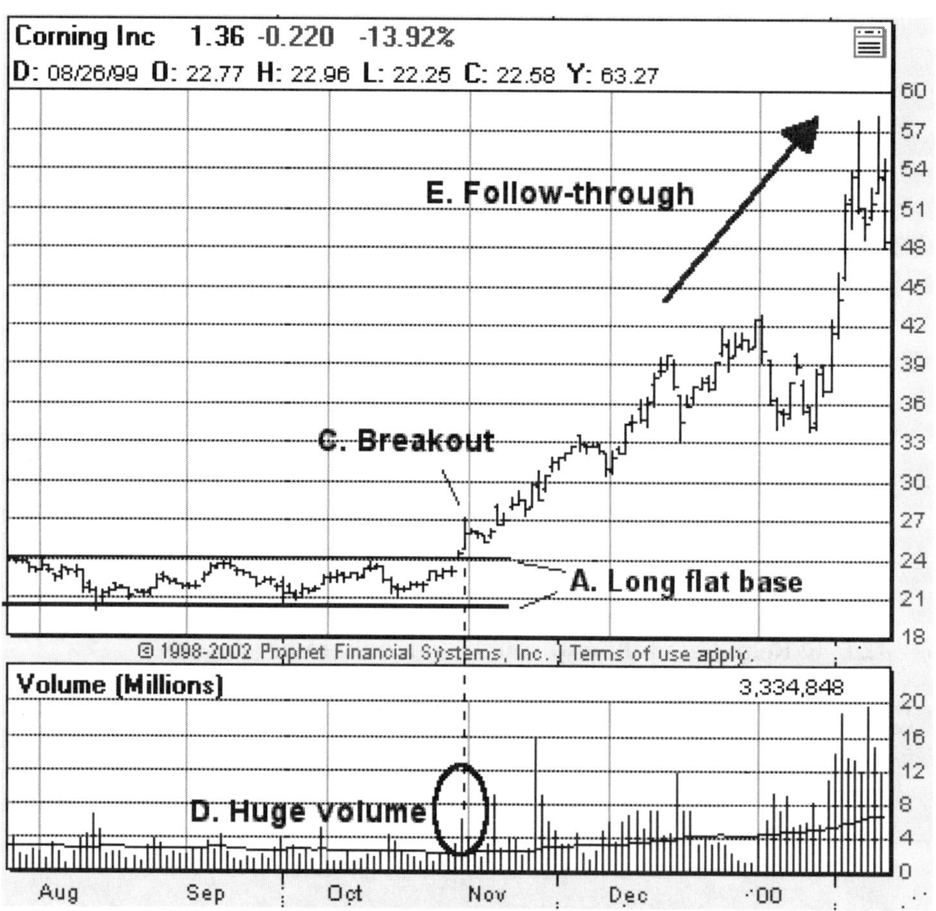

Figure 3-5

Reprinted courtesy of Prophet Financial Systems, Inc.—www.prophet.net

Here is excellent example in Corning (GLW).

- ☑ A: Long flat base of 3 months, more than our minimum of 8 weeks.
- ☐ B: We don't get our tightening of the short-term price action, but as I had mentioned, this is nice to have, but *not essential.*
- ☑ C: Price breaks out above the base.
- ☑ D. Huge volume.
- ☑ E: Relentless follow-through with only minor pauses.

If you had bought Corning at the time of the breakout, you would have been up over 100% in 3 months.

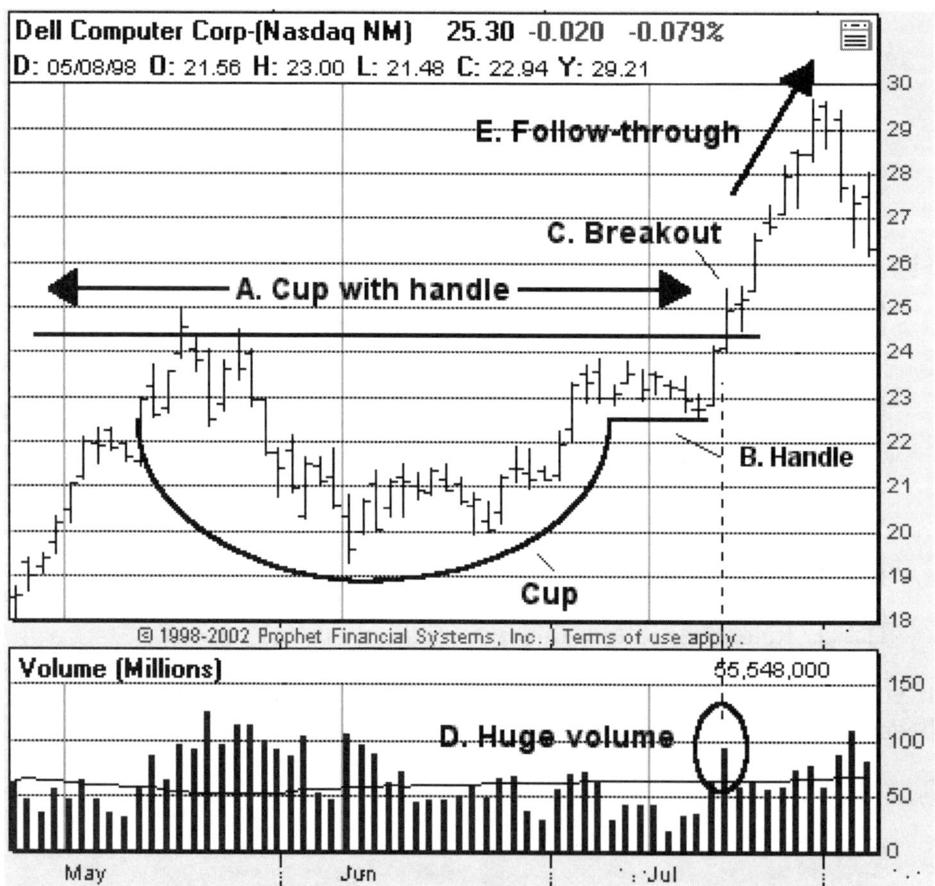

Figure 3-6

Reprinted courtesy of Prophet Financial Systems, Inc.—www.prophet.net

Here's Dell Computer (DELL) with a cup with handle formation.

- ☑ A: Cup with handle that is about 8 weeks in length, meeting our minimum requirement.
- ☑ B: The handle.
- ☑ C: Price breaks out above the upper resistence level of the cup with handle.
- ☑ D. Huge volume.
- ☑ E: Follow-through with only minor pauses. To show you the detail of the cup with handle, I didn't include much of the follow-through in the chart. But Dell was up over 100% over the course of the next 7 months.

WHY BREAKOUTS ARE KEY

While many technicians view breakouts as "just one of many" run-of-the-mill patterns, they have become my bread and butter. Certainly, I look at other chart patterns such as cup with handle and head and shoulders patterns, but breakouts when viewed in different contexts have an astonishingly wide variety of uses.

That will become increasingly apparent as I walk you through different components of my market analysis in later chapters. But briefly, here is what I have found to be the case through research of many years of data and studying thousands of charts.

- **The highest velocity and greatest momentum comes into a market or individual stock when it is breaking out cleanly from a sideways trading range.**

- **When breakouts occur on huge volume, they are, in my opinion, the lowest risk, highest-reward times at which to buy a stock** (or short it, if the market breaks down). In other words, when you get a solid breakout, the trend that ensues usually goes on for an extended period of time. If you get in at the beginning, you're home free.

Do you want to buy a stock at the beginning of a monstrous move? Most people can only recognize them after the fact. But I believe that breakouts allow you to capture these moves at the very beginning. Do you want to know why I have become even more confident of this recently? It's because at the time of this writing, we are in a bear market. There were many people who made money during the bull market and who stuck their chests out saying that they had the winning formula. Most of them are nowhere to be seen today because their methodologies were not robust enough to adapt to a bearish market environment.

WHAT ABOUT BREAKDOWNS?

Most traders don't trade the short side of the market. But they are missing out on great opportunities. A good example of this is the period between 2000 and 2002 in which a great deal of money was made as the market plummeted. I have a great way to capture gains as the market declines. *Because I want to fully ensure that you fully understand my unique shorting strategy, I devote my entire Chapter 8 to this topic.*

YOUR GAME PLAN FOR IDENTIFYING BREAKOUT SETUPS THAT CAN LEAD TO HUGE GAINS

Let's review. To find the best breakout setups:

☑ **A: Identify a base of 8 weeks or more in duration as taught in the previous chapter.** The longer and flatter the base, the better.

☑ **Look for a tightening of the trading range to occur over the course of 3 to 7 days whenever the price action rallies to resistance.** This is the clue that tells you that a breakout may be about to happen. *This short-term congestion isn't mandatory,* but when you see this little pattern you should immediately shift to high-alert status.

☑ **C: Watch for one day on which the price breaks above the base's resistance level.**

☑ **D: Make sure there is huge volume accompanying the breakout.** For small- to mid-cap stocks I need to see 2 to 3 times the average daily volume (averaged over the past 30 days). For bigger-cap stocks, 1.5 times the average daily volume will do the trick. The heavy volume indicates that institutions are heavily buying into the stock. That provides fuel for a long, extended rise.

☑ **E: Look for the price action that begins on the breakout day to be fast, explosive, and long-lasting.** If on the other hand, the breakout peters out within a few days, then something is wrong. I get out immediately. I don't even wait for my stop-loss to get hit (discussed in Chapter 9).

To find the best cup with handle setups:

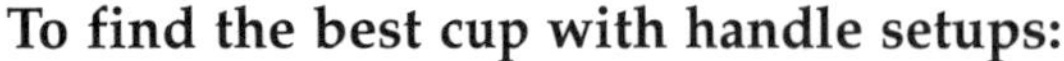

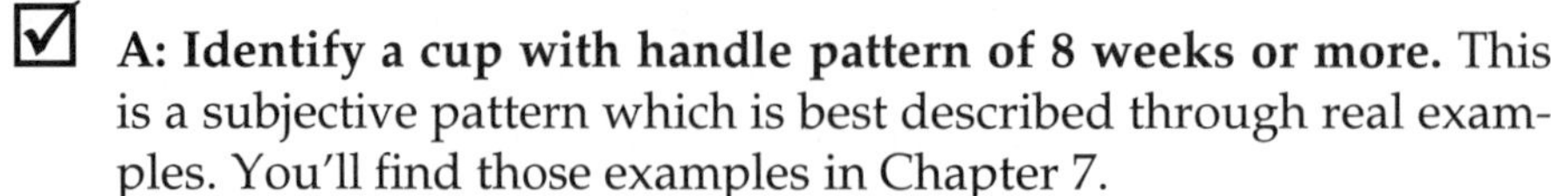

☑ **A: Identify a cup with handle pattern of 8 weeks or more.** This is a subjective pattern which is best described through real examples. You'll find those examples in Chapter 7.

☑ **B: Look for the "handle" which is a short-term tightening of the trading range over the course of 3 to 7 days as the right side of the pattern is formed.** This is the clue to look for that tells you that a breakout may be about to happen. When you see the handle, you should immediately shift to high-alert status.

☑ **C: Watch for one day on which the price breaks above the handle.**

☑ **D: Make sure there is huge volume accompanying the breakout.** For small- to mid-cap stocks I need to see 2 to 3 times the average daily volume (averaged over the past 30 days). For bigger-cap stocks, 1.5 times the average daily volume will do the trick.

☑ **E: Look for the price action that begins on the breakout day to be fast, explosive, and long-lasting.** As with breakouts from long flat bases, if the up-move peters out within a few days, then something is wrong. I get out immediately. I don't even wait for my stop-loss to get hit (discussed in Chapter 9).

In the next chapter, I will use everything I've taught you so far to show you how to time the markets.

PART II

Putting The Odds In Your Favor *Before You Buy Any Stock*

CHAPTER FOUR

How To Time The Market . . . *Without Predicting Anything*

It's sort of funny, but sad, to look back on conversations I overheard probably thousands of times when the bull market became a central fixation of public consciousness. People would stand in line in the late '90s signing up their kids for swim lessons talking about what stocks they were going to buy, without paying attention to the direction of the overall market, because they operated under the wrong assumption that a market that gained 20% or more a year was the norm. So, naturally, the reasoning was that a stock that had already risen 100% or 200% was going to go even higher. So, buy, buy, buy!

Well, the truth is that the market direction not only matters, but it is the single most important influence on the long-term direction of an individual stock. That is not only true today, but it has always been so.

So, the bottom line is:

> When you see a great breakout setup, you must make sure that the direction of the overall market is going to help and not hinder you. *In Chapter 9 on Nighty Preparation, you will learn how to integrate market timing with stock selection.*

In this chapter I will teach you the process by which I formulate an intelligent bias on the likely direction of the market. Because I am not in the entertainment business or pretend to be a psychic, I do not use the information I gather to *predict* anything about the future. So, not only can I quickly change my opinion if the technical circumstances change, but I also consciously start each day anew knowing that I have to go down the checklist again and determine what the new day's market direction will probably be.

Yes, I know you can split hairs and say, well, if I have any opinion at all, aren't I predicting something? I would argue that people who predict the markets are committing themselves publicly to an opinion about the future. I never commit myself or become emotionally attached to any opinion at any given time. I have been on TV shows where I frustrate the heck out of the hosts because I refuse to cave into comforting people with a false sense of certainty about the future. I just give them the facts and tell them what I think the market is saying today, knowing full well that tomorrow I have to re-evaluate everything.

HOW TO DETERMINE TODAY'S MARKET DIRECTION

Every day I reassess the market and arrive at one of the following simple conclusions:

- The market is now going up.
- The market is now going down.
- The market is going sideways.

It is crucial for you to understand how important it is not only to be flexible and ready to change your opinion from moment to moment, but also not to have an opinion when technical clues are hazy or inconclusive. This will keep you out of trouble.

In order to arrive at the above conclusions, let me give you a brief overview of the market timing checklist that works for me. *Then, I will go into detail, teaching you how to use each tool I mention in the checklist.*

☑ **1. Determine the number and quality of breakouts you see in the major indices, sectors, and individual stocks.**

- The more big breakouts to the upside with follow-through you see, the more **bullish** you should become.
- The more big breakouts to the downside (breakdowns) with follow-through you see, the more **bearish** you should become.

☑ **2. Check if there is leadership in the market.**

- If you see high profile stocks making new highs day after day and week after week, that's **bullish.**
- If you see high profile stocks breaking down or making new lows day after day and week after week, that's **bearish.**

☑ **3. Determine whether the sentiment of the public and Wall Street "experts" has reached a bullish or bearish extreme.**

- When they are excessively bullish, you should be bearish or at least ready to turn **bearish.**
- When they are excessively bearish, you should be bullish or at least ready to turn **bullish.**

☑ **4. Check the 50-day and 200-day moving averages in the major indices and individual stocks.**

- If the major indices and many stocks are trading below them, that's a confirmation that you're in a **bear market.**
- If the major indices and many stocks are trading above them, that's a confirmation that you're in a **bull market.**

☑ 5. **Look at long-term charts to determine where the market is in the context of past bull and bear markets.** By doing this, you can gain a very rough idea how close you are on the current day to the beginning or end of a **bull** or **bear** market.

☑ 6. **Check for evidence of institutional buying or selling** by looking for volume accumulation or distribution in the major indices and individual stocks.

- When you see a lot of accumulation, that's **bullish.**
- When you see a lot of distribution, that's **bearish.**

☑ 7. **Keep your eyes open for O'Neil Follow-Through Days during major market declines.** Many major market bottoms of the past have coincided with this pattern.

Now let's walk through each of these indicators:

1. DETERMINE THE NUMBER AND QUALITY OF BREAKOUTS YOU SEE IN THE MAJOR INDICES, SECTORS, AND INDIVIDUAL STOCKS

You and I cannot read the mind of the market. So we have to look for clues by analyzing what the market is doing now and what it has done in the recent past. From there, you can formulate an intelligent opinion about whether or not today is a good day to be buying stocks.

My simple observation of price action and volume involves looking at thousands of charts each evening after the markets close. I use Daily Graphs Online for this (see Appendix for subscription information). What am I mainly looking for?

You guessed it: *Breakouts!*

Here is how you can make an excellent assessment of the health of the market move based upon this marvelous pattern. You just look at . . .

- **Breakouts in the major market indices.** When you see the Dow, S&P 500 and Nasdaq breaking above a major resistance level on heavy volume after having traded in a range for several weeks, it's a sign that the market could launch into a powerful rally, but . . .

- If you see those three key indices breaking down below a major support level on heavy volume, it's a sign that the market is in trouble and could head considerably lower.

- **The direction of breakouts in individual stocks.**

  - If you see many stocks breaking out on monster volume from the tops of trading ranges and then going higher, *the market itself is likely to be headed higher.* This can be a leading indicator. In other words, you may see the indices doing very little or acting somewhat negative. But breakouts in many individual stocks is a sign of strength that may eventually push the market higher.

  - If you see *many stocks breaking down on monster volume from the bottoms of trading ranges and then going lower, the market itself is likely to be headed lower.* Again, it can be a leading indicator if you do not yet see the same action reflected in the indices.

- **The quantity of breakouts among individual stocks and sectors.**

  - The more stocks and the more industry groups you see breaking out on monster volume in one direction, *the stronger the market move is likely to be in the direction of the breakout.* If you see the market indices rally strongly, but the breakouts in individual stocks are practically non-existent, that rally is on thin ice.

- **The quality of breakouts among individual stocks and sectors.**

  - After you see a lot of stocks breaking out higher and a market rally ensues, are you continuing to see stocks going higher and higher day after day? That's a sign that the overall market has the momentum and strength to keep on going. If, on the other hand, you see many stocks plummeting and then reversing back downward, it's a sign that the market is weak and vulnerable.

Now let's look at some charts as I show you how breakouts can help you anticipate major market turns.

Here is a classic example of a breakout in EMC Corp that occurred in early 1998. It traded in a range for 15 weeks, forming what I call a "base." Then it broke out from the top of the base on huge volume. From there, the stock never looked back, and it scored a 500% gain from that breakout.

Figure 4-1 Reprinted courtesy of Prophet Financial Systems, Inc.—www.prophet.net

During the same period from January until the middle of 1998 you had other stocks like . . .

. . . Microsoft (MSFT) and . . .

Figure 4-2

Reprinted courtesy of Prophet Financial Systems, Inc.—www.prophet.net

. . . Yahoo (YHOO) and many other key technology stocks like Intel (INTC), Oracle (ORCL), Cisco (CSCO) and Sun Microsystems (SUNW) *doing the same thing!*

Figure 4-3 Reprinted courtesy of Prophet Financial Systems, Inc.—www.prophet.net

And look what that told you!

Figure 4-4 Reprinted courtesy of Prophet Financial Systems, Inc.—www.prophet.net

The breakouts in individual technology stocks in late 1998 and through 1999 told you that the Nasdaq, which was made up of many technology companies, was going to have a big year. It didn't take anything approaching rocket science to see this happen and not only catch the move in individual stocks, but also in the market itself.

And indeed that is how it played out, as you can see in this chart of the Nasdaq in which the widely followed index gained over 100% in a year.

And now get this . . . some of you who know market history may be muttering to yourselves, "Yeah, but it all ended in 2000 when the market plummeted into an abyss. Where was your breakout market-timing system then?"

> **I'll tell you. The same approach of monitoring breakouts told me quite clearly that the market was topping out in March and April of 2000. While many others were saying that we were witnessing a temporary pullback in a bull market, the large number of breakdowns across a broad base of sectors told me that the market was in trouble.**

2. CHECK IF THERE IS LEADERSHIP IN THE MARKET

Besides breakouts on heavy volume, I would rank leadership as being neck and neck in importance in determining market strength or weakness.

You need to see leadership in any bull market or major rally.

Any bull market or major rally that has no leadership is standing on thin ice.

> To determine whether any major rally or bull market has the legs to keep going for a decent enough time for you to be looking for opportunities in individual stocks, you have to look at what the big names are doing.
>
> **They are the leaders and the rest of the market follows them!**

Leadership simply refers to the fact that real bull markets always have a strong core group of quality big-name stocks which are pushing continually to new 12-month highs, or that are in strong uptrends and are trading within 10% of their 12-month highs. Want a good example of leadership?

Just look at the stocks I've already shown you, like EMC, Microsoft and Yahoo in Figures 4-1, 4-2 and 4-3. Also look at . . .

. . . what appear to be carbon copies of the same breakout pattern in stocks such as Intel (INTC) . . .

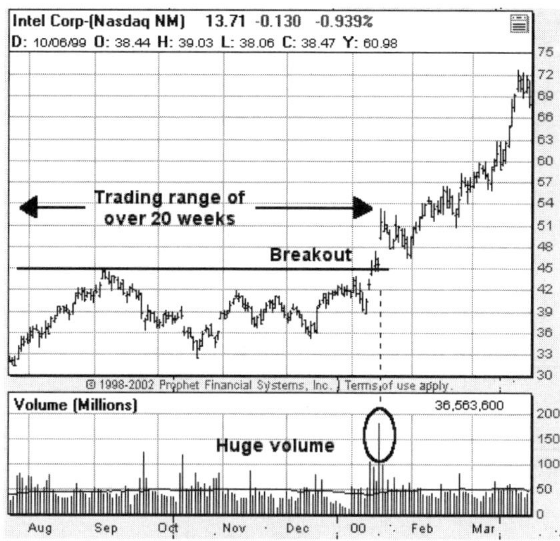

Figure 4-5 Reprinted courtesy of Prophet Financial Systems, Inc.—www.prophet.net

. . . Sun Microsystems (SUNW) and . . .

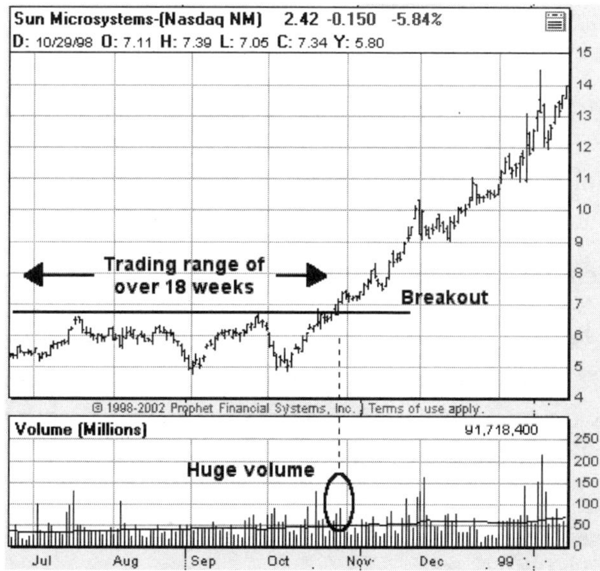

Figure 4-6 Reprinted courtesy of Prophet Financial Systems, Inc.—www.prophet.net

. . . Broadcom (BRCM)

Figure 4-7

Reprinted courtesy of Prophet Financial Systems, Inc.—www.prophet.net

You can study the charts of these stocks and dozens of others that were leaders in late 1998 and early 1999. You will notice that these stocks were continually making new highs. That was telling you that the rally in the market was for real and had legs.

That is what leadership is all about.

> An often-asked question is: "What is going to lead the next bull market?" I can't answer this because I don't know. But to help you narrow down your list of leaders, plus enable you to properly use the leadership indicator, let me give you some rules of thumb.

All of the following research can be performed using Daily Graphs, Daily Graphs Online, or Investors Business Daily. *Information about these resources is available in the Appendix.* **My rules of thumb in using the leadership indicator are:**

- **To determine which stocks are likely to provide leadership for the rest of the market, you have to look at what industries are playing the biggest role in fueling economic growth.** You especially want to focus on this during the earlier phase of a rally or full-fledged bull market. When I see a rally in the major stock indices such as the S&P and Nasdaq, I look at certain sectors that have always done well at the start of new bull markets. These are the ones in the top 25% of all industry groups. Among my favorites are Financials, Retailers and Technology. The leaders to follow are those stocks which are outdoing their competitors and whose earnings, sales and market cap reflect that. You don't have to be a bean counter to figure out who the leaders are. Just look at which companies are making the headlines in the news media. Keep asking yourself : "Who are the movers and shakers that people view as models of success?"

- **When you see a market rally accompanied by big-name growth stocks making new highs, the market has strong leadership.** This is an indication that the market itself has strength and that it's a good environment for buying stocks.

- **When you see a market rally in the major indices, but all you see are failed breakouts or poor performance among the big-name stocks, then I would call it a fragile rally**, and I'd be sitting on the sidelines or looking for candidates to short once the rally peters out.

- **Leadership begets leadership.** When you see leaders behaving strongly week after week, it not only tells you that the market is strong, but also that there is momentum to drive the market even higher . . . as long as the leadership persists. But watch out when the leadership begins to cave in. If that happens, the rest of the market is likely to follow.

- **Remember also that laggards beget laggards.** If the market is dropping like a rock and you see those inevitable rally attempts, be sure to see if leadership kicks in. If it doesn't, no matter how strong the rally in the Dow, S&P or Nasdaq looks, don't trust it. These kinds of rally attempts in the midst of a bear market tend to drag in a lot of suckers, but are usually quite short-lived. Keeping track of how leaders are plummeting during a bear market is a great way to determine whether the market is ripe for shorting stocks.

- **Keep your eyes on what type of stocks and industry groups are leading.**

  - If gold is leading and everything else is trashed, it's telling you something bad is going on.
  - Sectors that always lead in good markets include the Financials, Retailers and Technology.
  - If homebuilders and financials are getting whacked, it may mean that interest rates are going up.
  - If homebuilders and financials are going up, it may mean that the interest rates are going down.
  - Utilities notoriously do poorly in a bad interest-rate environment and do well in a good interest-rate environment because they are borrowers of money. And if interest rates come down, the cost of capital comes down and that goes right to their bottom line.

3. DETERMINE WHETHER THE SENTIMENT OF THE PUBLIC AND WALL STREET "EXPERTS" HAS REACHED A BULLISH OR BEARISH EXTREME

Sentiment is a favorite technical tool of mine which looks closely at people's emotions. It works best when the market is moving widely in one direction, driving either fear or greed into the hearts of traders. The raw mechanics of sentiment are as follows:

- Market bottoms tend to occur when fear dominates the minds of the trading public to the point where hardly anybody wants to buy stocks anymore.

- Market tops tend to occur when everybody is so confident that the market will keep going higher that they get greedy and buy stocks recklessly.

Before I get into the details, it's important to point out that sentiment should always be used in combination with other market-timing tools such as price action, volume and leadership (discussed earlier). That's because sentiment doesn't come in the form of a crisp signal that incites me to action. Rather, sentiment, when manifested in the form of extreme levels of fear or greed, *sets the stage* for a big move. I have to see the bigger technical picture fall into place before I can take action. Something has to trigger the move that sentiment tells me the market is in danger of making. So think of extreme readings in sentiment as an alarm bell that puts you in a heightened state of alert.

The use of sentiment is both an art and a science. Let's talk about each separately.

The *Art* Of Using Sentiment To Time The Markets

Note: The strategy I am about to teach you is very, very subjective and is not designed to provide you with a precise buy or sell signal. But I think it is beneficial to intertwine real-life observations with indicators such as Put/Call ratios.

I am a big believer in getting an overall feel for the market by simply looking at people, watching what they do, and listening to what they say. Instead of being a member of the crowd, stand outside of "group-think" and observe what the crowd is doing.

While I have an edge in that every day I am able to sample a cross-section of humanity through my nationally syndicated radio show, you can still make these observations in the normal course of your daily routine.

Observations that tell me that a significant low in the market *may* set up soon include:

- When I see pain on many people's faces when they are losing money. Keep in mind that in a bullish environment, people are oblivious to losing money because they think that next week the market will recover and they'll get it all back, and more!

- When I hear people talk about how their retirement funds have been decimated and how they have no hope whatsoever left in the stock market.

- When 40 people call me on my radio show asking me what stocks to short.

- When the news media can do nothing but report bad news that scares the heck out of the average person. Back at the lows in 1998, I was listening to rumors of Banker's Trust and Lehman Brothers filing bankruptcy. I was listening to the supposed destruction of the finance system because of a hedge fund, with Russia and Mexico imploding. Well, at that time, the charts of stocks like Microsoft, Yahoo and EMC, as well as the scores of other stocks I mentioned earlier in this chapter, were revving up to blast the Nasdaq up over 100% in 1999. Get it? So when all they talk about is depression, recession, how the U.S. is going to be the next Japan, layoffs, bankruptcies, analyst downgrades, lowered estimates, no visibility, stagflation, etc., just remember that this kind of talk occurs near market lows.

But when I see the following, I will be alert for the market to top out:

- Glee on people's faces when they are making money and buying more and more stock. In a bearish environment in which people have been pummeled to the limit, when people see the market go up, they are pessimistic and use it as an opportunity to dump stock.

- Desperate urgency of people asking me what stocks to buy. If I tell them that the timing isn't right or to wait for better market conditions, they get mad because their neighbor's portfolio is up a lot more than theirs.

- Somebody comes to my office and tells me that they expect their account to be up 40% this year and they stomp out mad when I tell them that I can guarantee it *won't*.

- People do ridiculous things like attach Quotron machines to their dashboards, have their online brokerage order entry screen up all day at work, or set up 18 monitors in their home in order to monitor stock charts and financial news.

- Near market highs, the news media reports on a wide range of things that defy common sense, you name it: seven-year old kids with six-figure portfolios; companies making triple-digit gains in spite of having no earnings now or in the foreseeable future, and every news show with financial reporters making stock picks. I could go on and on because the scenario is so fresh in my mind!

Even though I come into contact with people throughout the country on a daily basis through my radio show, through message boards on my subscription service, and the e-mail I receive from many people who read my column at TradingMarkets.com, don't think of yourself as being at a disadvantage in making the observations that I make. You can stay in tune with sentiment by monitoring the emotion of the people you come into contact with at work, and among your friends and family members.

The *Science* Of Using Sentiment To Time The Markets

There are also quantitative approaches to reading sentiment. Here are my favorites:

Investors Intelligence Tells The Story

At the end of 1999 and the beginning of 2000, the Nasdaq was cooking.

Biotechs, Internets and Technology seemingly could not be stopped. Bullishness in the market was running rampant. Investors' expectations were sky high and rising. Analysts had recommendations with targets of four figures. Newsletter writers were telling you to back up the truck.

Fast-forward to February 2001. The Dow and S&P 500 had sustained intermediate-term corrections. The Nasdaq was down a whopping 53% from its March 2000 high. Many famous tech names were down more than 70% and a bunch of Internets had already said bye-bye.

You would have expected them to have much less optimism in the markets. In fact, you would expect downright pessimism. But these talking bulls hadn't budged.

One of the most popular gauges of sentiment, and my favorite, comes from a company called Investors Intelligence (see the Appendix for subscription information). This company tracks newsletter writers. Many years ago, Investors Intelligence decided to follow these writers' opinions in order to decipher which way the market was headed. They figured that if all these writers were bullish, it would be a good sign to be in the market. Were they in for a surprise! After years of study, they found the polar opposite was true. It turned out that these writers were trend followers and would only turn bullish or bearish *after* the move.

Thus, I consider the bullish newsletter number a great *contrarian* indicator. In the past, when optimism has gone to extremes, it often preceded market tops. When pessimism hit extremes, it often signaled a bottom.

55% or higher bulls is bearish

35% bulls is bullish

Most people believe it is a mistake to watch these numbers. I disagree. While I will always believe market action holds the most weight, when these numbers go to extremes, they have worked quite well for me as a secondary indicator of where the market cycle might be.

Figure 4-8 Reprinted courtesy of Prophet Financial Systems, Inc.—www.prophet.net

Here are some facts to chew on:

Throughout the major drop of March 2000 until February 2001, the newsletter writers stayed steadfastly bullish. At the beginning of February 2001, and not so coincidentally after the move up, the bulls hit 61.8%, a 14-year high. I viewed this as a worrisome number and rightly so. From February 2001 until late 2002, the S&P 500 declined nearly 40%!

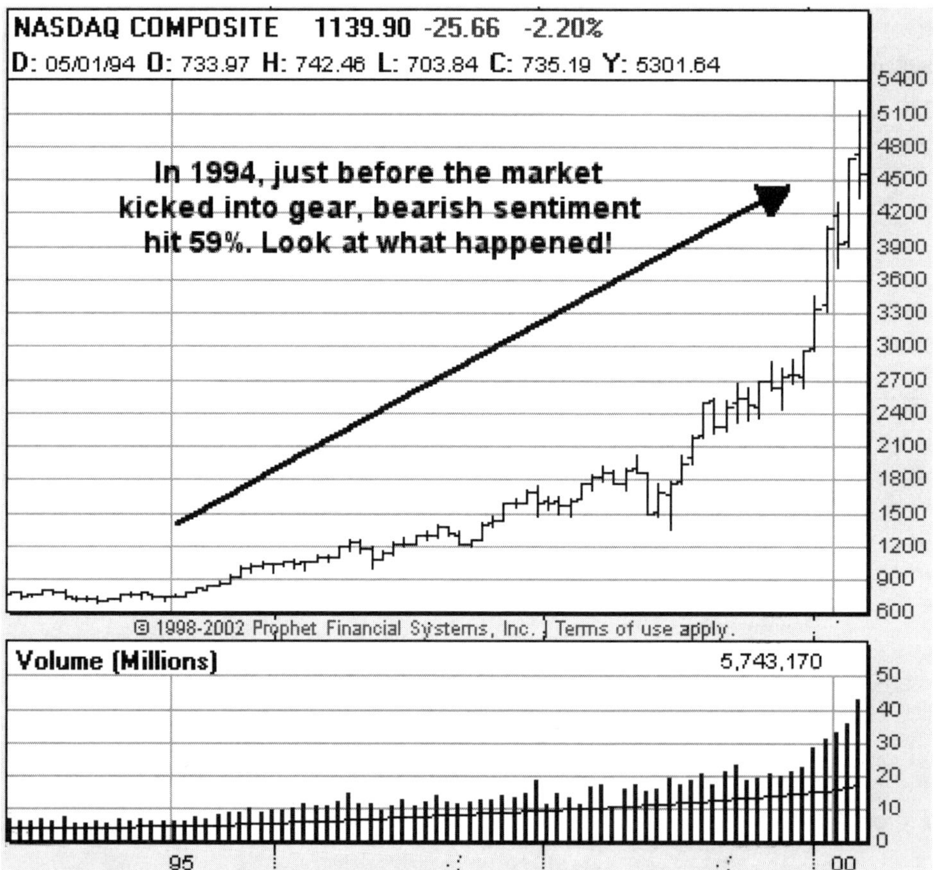

Figure 4-9 Reprinted courtesy of Prophet Financial Systems, Inc.—www.prophet.net

In 1994, just before the market kicked into gear, bearish sentiment hit 59%. The market catapulted almost straight up for the next six years!

Figure 4-10 Reprinted courtesy of Prophet Financial Systems, Inc.—www.prophet.net

In 1987, 61% of advisors were bullish all the way into October right up to the crash!

These are just a few moments in history when these numbers went to extremes. Keep in mind, these extremes do not happen very often. I urge you to start paying close attention to this indicator and watch for these extremes. You can find this number every day on the "Big Picture" page of *Investors Business Daily.*

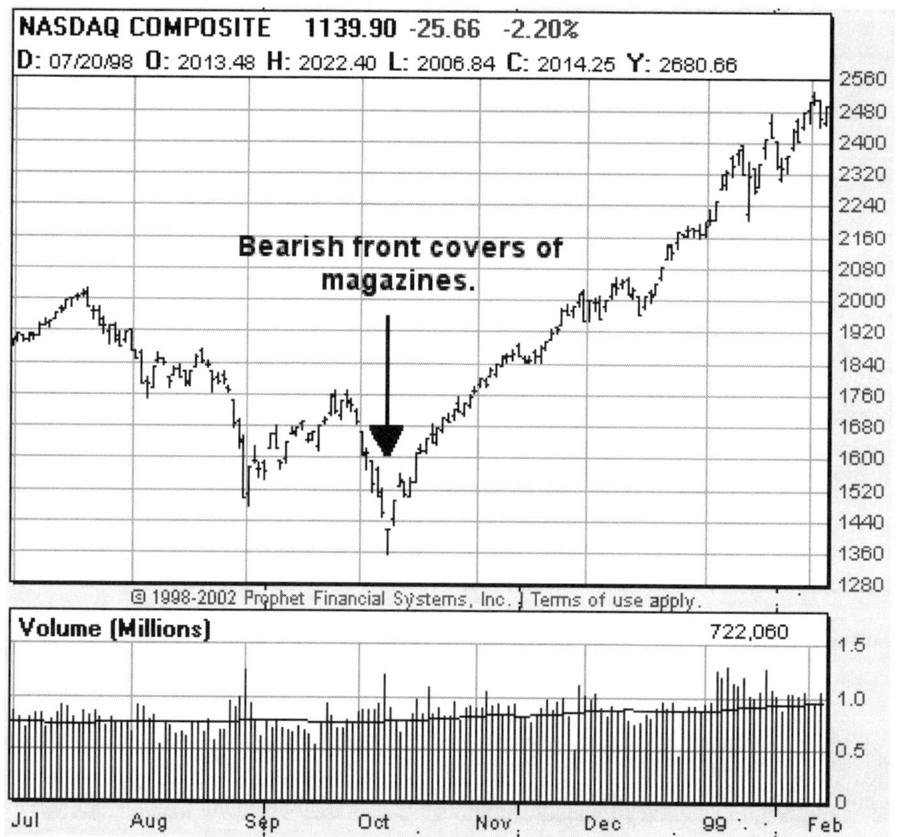

Figure 4-11 Reprinted courtesy of Prophet Financial Systems, Inc. -- www.prophet.net

The Front Cover Indicator

The Front Cover Indicator is fun, but one which is nevertheless important to keep track of. This works better during bear markets at hinting at major lows than it does in bull markets suggesting the market is topping out. Back at the **'98 lows,** *Newsweek, Time, Fortune, Forbes,* and even *Esquire* had front covers depicting crashes and bears. Of course, this happened after the drop. These magazines are notorious in reporting the news loudly after the move has already been made. Pictures of bears and declining charts in *Newsweek, Time, U.S. News* and *The Economist* get me wondering whether a major rally is ahead.

OTHER MARKET TIMING INDICATORS

I use a variety of other market timing indicators which I'll describe briefly. I won't go into full detail about them right now because I want you to maintain your focus on the big-picture tools. If you want to gain a professional level of knowledge and expertise, resources are provided at the end of this book.

4. CHECK THE 50-DAY AND 200-DAY MOVING AVERAGES IN THE MAJOR INDICES AND INDIVIDUAL STOCKS

A lot of people use moving averages. Maybe that's why they work! In any event, the fact is that you can identify price levels at which major market turns could potentially occur by looking at two major moving averages, the 50-day and 200-day simple moving averages. Many big Wall Street institutions track these and tend to move in and out of the market when they are penetrated or touched. So it's a good thing to monitor as you are doing your nightly research in the comfort of your living room. Simple rules of thumb:

When you've been in a major bull market, but you see the S&P 500, Dow Jones Industrial Average, Nasdaq, sectors and big-name stocks breaking below their 50-day moving averages, a serious correction or transition to a bear market may be occurring.

And when you see them all breaking below their 200-day moving averages . . . it's curtains—as the market is drifting into serious bear territory.

But the good news is when you see the opposite occur during a bear market, it's an indication that a new bull market is under development.

A nice tactic that follows the same principle as breakout pattern techniques is to watch for many stocks and sectors all hitting the same moving average simultaneously. It happens more often than you might think. If you see numerous stocks and sectors breaking below their 50-day moving averages for example, get out of the way. The market could stage a major acceleration to the downside. On the other hand, if you see everything breaking above the 50-day (or 200-day for that matter) moving average, you might see a major rally ensue.

These moving averages can be found on most major market analysis web sites, as well as software charting tools.

5. LOOK AT LONG-TERM CHARTS TO DETERMINE WHERE THE MARKET IS IN THE CONTEXT OF PAST BULL AND BEAR MARKETS

I believe an awareness of long-term cycles can prevent a lot of heartache as well as help keep your awareness from being clouded by the mob mentality. By long-term cycles, I am referring to the rhythm and pace of past major market trends. Understanding this helps you answer the question: How much like today will tomorrow be?

Keep things like this in mind: You had an 18-year bull market going into 1966, you had from '66-'82 nothing, and from '82 to 2000, another 18 years. If the past is any indication, the bear market that started in early 2000 may be the beginning of a multi-year stage. I won't predict that this will be the case, but you have to recognize that this is how it works. The time is ripe for a long, protracted bear market cycle . . . a flat period like the one we had from '66 to '82 . . . in which there were mini-bear markets and mini-bull markets. Sixteen years of blah!

Still, let me not cast a dark shadow on your investment portfolio. You can make money during these periods!

6. CHECK FOR EVIDENCE OF INSTITUTIONAL BUYING OR SELLING

For my analysis, volume comes into play big time when a breakout is occurring. But there are subtle clues that you can watch for when a long trading range or base is being formed. These will help you to see: a) whether a breakout will actually take place, and b) whether it will occur to the upside or downside. What you look at are accumulation days and distribution days.

An accumulation day occurs when a stock closes higher and the day's volume is higher than the prior day's volume. This tells you that institutions are buying and that's bullish.

A distribution day occurs when a stock closes lower and the day's volume is higher than the prior day's volume. This tells you that the institutions are selling and that's bearish.

If, in the midst of a stock bouncing aimlessly in a trading range over the course of many weeks or months, you see many accumulation days, it's an indication that one day the stock may break out and explode higher.

But if you see many distribution days during that base building, you may very well see a breakdown to lower price levels instead.

7. KEEP YOUR EYES OPEN FOR O'NEIL FOLLOW-THROUGH DAYS DURING MAJOR MARKET DECLINES

Bull markets tend to start with a big rally. During the first week, you'll see **a day with at least a 1% to 2% gain on heavier volume than the previous day.** That's called a follow-through day. It's important to note that not all follow-though days usher in bull markets. So, use this indicator as a confirmation, not as a signal to buy everything in sight.

YOUR GAME PLAN FOR DETERMINING THE CURRENT MARKET DIRECTION

OK, let's sum up what I've taught you in this chapter.

Buying or selling stocks that move in sync with the market gives you a tremendous edge. To determine which direction the current market is moving in, do the following:

☑ **1. Determine the number and quality of breakouts you see in the major indices, sectors, and individual stocks.**

- The more big breakouts to the upside with follow-through you see, the more **bullish** you should be become.
- The more big breakouts to the downside (breakdowns) with follow-through you see, the more **bearish** you should become.

☑ 2. **Check if there is leadership in the market.**

- If you see high profile stocks making new highs day after day and week after week, that's **bullish**.

- If you see high profile stocks breaking down or making new lows day after day and week after week, that's **bearish.**

☑ **3. Determine whether the sentiment of the public and Wall Street "experts" has reached a bullish or bearish extreme.**

- When they are excessively bullish, you should be bearish or at least ready to turn **bearish.**

- When they are excessively bearish, you should be bullish or at least ready to turn **bullish.**

☑ **4. Check the 50-day and 200-day moving averages in the major indices and individual stocks.**

- If the major indices and many stocks are trading below them, that's a confirmation that you're in **bear market.**

- If the major indices and many stocks are trading above them, that's a confirmation that you're in **bull market.**

☑ **5. Look at long-term charts to determine where the market is in the context of past bull and bear markets.** By doing this you can gain a very rough idea how close you are on the current day to the beginning or end of a **bull** or **bear** market.

☑ **6. Check for evidence of institutional buying or selling** by looking for volume accumulation or distribution in the major indices and individual stocks.

- When you see a lot of accumulation, that's **bullish.**

- When you see a lot of distribution, that's **bearish.**

☑ **7. Keep your eyes open for O'Neil Follow-Through Days during major market declines.** Many major market bottoms of the past have coincided with this pattern.

I gave you the basics of how to look at charts in Chapter 2 and then explained my key chart pattern, breakouts, in Chapter 3. And in this chapter, now ending, I have explained how to apply breakouts and other technical tools to timing the market as a whole.

We have started to lay the groundwork for the successful buying and selling of stocks. In the next chapter, we'll take a close look at how focusing on industry groups and sectors can help you find winning stocks in both bull and bear markets.

CHAPTER FIVE

What's The Fastest Way To Find Winning Stocks?

These days, no matter what business you're in, everybody perks up when you can offer instant gratification. In developing my investment methodology, I have striven to find a formula that would deliver results. Getting there requires hard work and the real payoff can take months to years to happen. But, if there was one aspect of the craft I am teaching you that I am tempted to characterize as "fast and easy," it would be the use of industry groups to find the best buying and shorting candidates in the market.

Here are the general characteristics of industry groups that you'll learn to put to practical use:

> The stock market is made up of stocks whose underlying companies do business in a wide range of industries. *The stocks belonging to specific industry groups tend to move together like schools of fish.* Different industry groups lead the market at different times. Over the course of several months, the Semiconductor stocks may dominate. Stocks within that group are making

new highs every day. Then at some point, they get knocked out of the leadership position and perhaps the oils become king of the hill. And the whole process continues as different groups jostle for leadership. It pays to keep track of the rotation of industry group leadership. Why? Because **the movement of individual stocks belonging to each industry group is greatly influenced by the movement of the group.**

This leads me to the next piece of my Methodology I want to teach you.

HOW TO FIND BREAKOUT SETUPS THAT HAVE THE BEST ODDS OF LAUNCHING INTO MONSTER MOVES

If you want the odds stacked in your favor when you buy or short stocks, here's what you do:

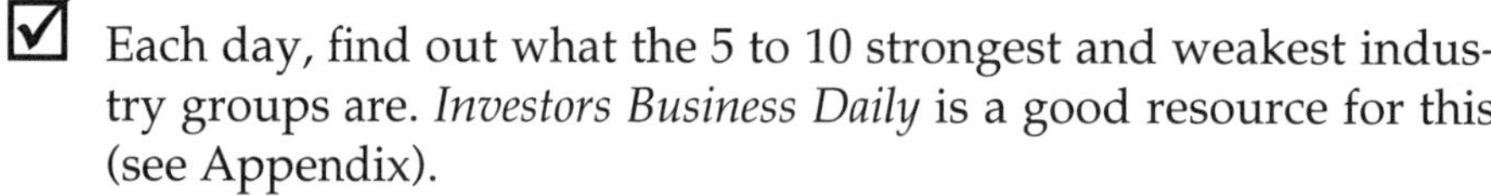

- ☑ Each day, find out what the 5 to 10 strongest and weakest industry groups are. *Investors Business Daily* is a good resource for this (see Appendix).
- ☑ If you want to find breakout setups that have the best odds of launching into monster up-moves, look for them in the **strongest industry groups.**
- ☑ If you want to find breakdown setups that have the best odds of launching into monster **down-moves**, look for them in the **weakest industry groups**.
- ☑ Be on the lookout for new emerging industry group leaders (both strong and weak) that move up in the rankings. Monitor these groups for breakout and breakdown candidates that may bear fruit if these groups jump to the top rankings.

Let me give you some real-life examples of how industry group awareness provides you with a great edge. *While these examples show you how industry groups can sometimes exert a greater influence over the movement of individual stocks than the overall market, I want to emphasize that when we put all the pieces of my Methodology together in Chapter 6, ideally, both the market and the industry group should be in sync.*

You remember this "delightful" moment in market history don't you? Note that the highs occurred in March 2000.

Figure 5-1 Reprinted courtesy of Prophet Financial Systems, Inc.—www.prophet.net

Well, here's an index which shows what was happening in the homebuilder industry. Pay careful attention to the lows of this index which occurred in March 2000, *the point at which the Nasdaq made its final highs.* Also, move your eyes over to the breakout noted on 8/07/00. What happened next was astonishing.

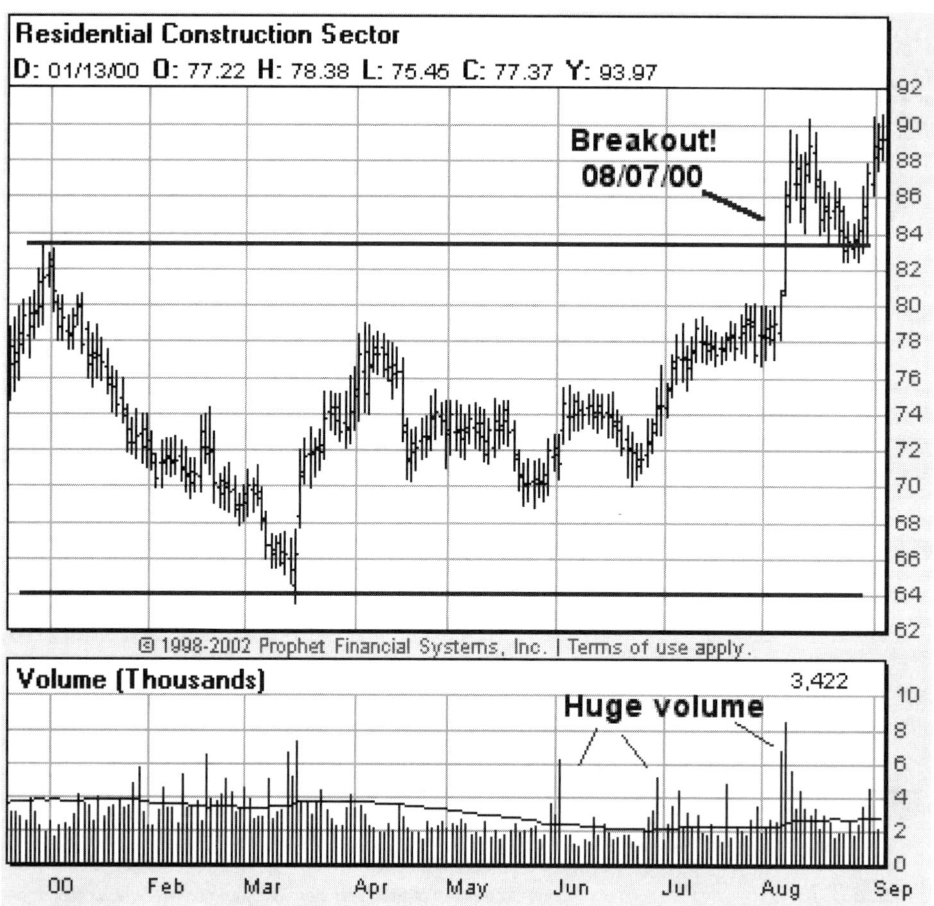

Figure 5-2

Reprinted courtesy of Prophet Financial Systems, Inc.—www.prophet.net

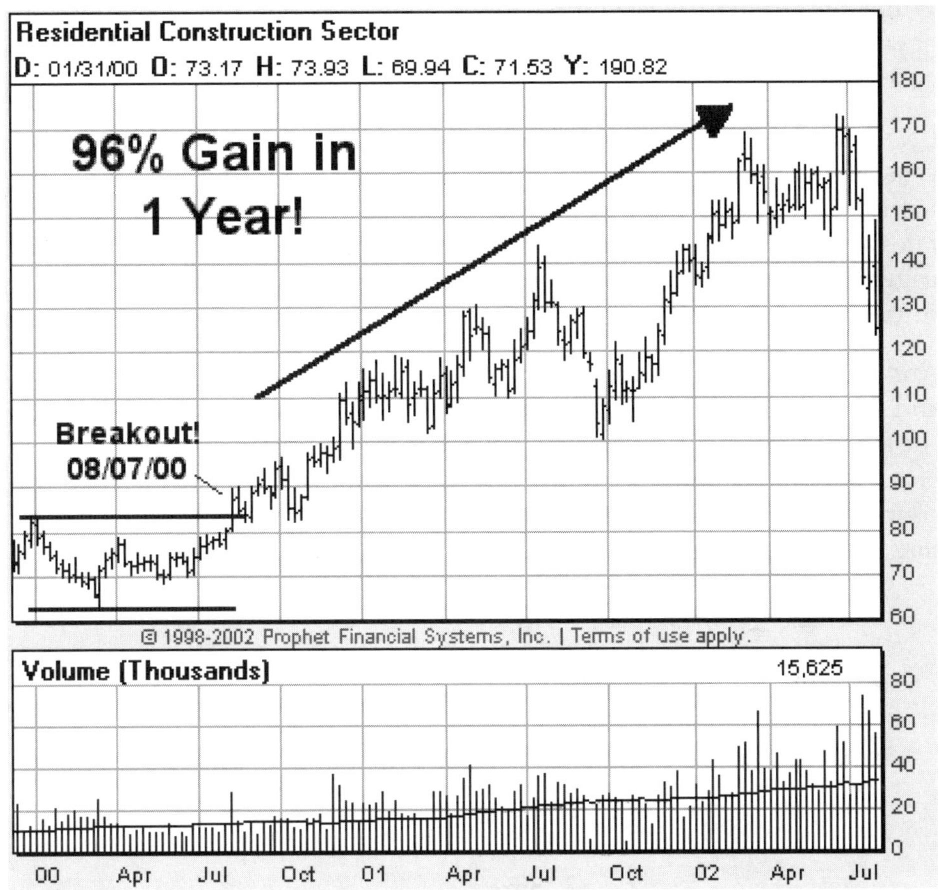

Figure 5-3 Reprinted courtesy of Prophet Financial Systems, Inc.—www.prophet.net

During the period of time between April and July 2000, following our checklist:

- ☑ You notice that the homebuilders are busting into the top industry group rankings.
- ☑ You go on the lookout for stocks in that industry category building long flat bases and gearing up for potential breakouts.

And here's what happened:

While the Nasdaq was getting killed, the homebuilders catapulted to new highs, giving you a "hidden" bull market by nearly doubling in a year.

I say "hidden" because most of the financial press were still fixated on yesterday's names, the JDS Uniphases, Broadcoms and Ciscos of the world. Yes, there's some economic background to this, in that interest rates were lowered down to a level not seen since the early '60s and this triggered growth in the housing market. But I really don't care. I just let price and volume tell me what to do.

And in this case, they were telling me to forget about yesterday's names and buy stocks of companies that built homes. What were the stocks that were really hot at the time? If you'd been watching the Homebuilder sector, you could have seen a lot of "ka-chings" over the course of the next year and half among stocks in the same group. I call these "cousin stocks" because they're in the same industries.

- Beazer Homes (BZH)—**Up 286%**
- Centex (CTX)—**Up 110%**
- Dominion (DHOM)—**Up 329%**
- Lennar Corp (LEN)—**Up 122%**
- Hovnanian (HOV)—**Up 394%**

Let's look at another example of the power of industry group analysis. The Aerospace/Defense group took off according to the classic breakout criteria.

Figure 5-4 Reprinted courtesy of Prophet Financial Systems, Inc.—www.prophet.net

Again you follow the textbook and you're doing your checklist in early 2002.

☑ You notice that the major defense contractor group is picking up steam and rising to the top of the rankings.

☑ You go on the lookout for stocks in that industry category building long flat bases and gearing up for potential breakouts.

And here's what happened:

It was a fast gain in a short amount of time, and you could have been there without having to interpret how defense contractors were going to benefit from the war on terrorism while talk of war with Iraq was going on. No . . . the entire story was once again in the chart itself.

And what do you do with this kind of information? Well, during this period, you could have bought cousin stocks like these:

- Boeing (BA)—**Up 25%** in two months.
- General Dynamics—(GD): **Up 28%** in six months
- Lockheed Martin (LMT)—**Up 42%** in six months
- Northrop Grumman (NOC)—**Up 26%** in six months
- Raytheon (RTN)—**Up 27%** in five months

YOUR GAME PLAN FOR IDENTIFYING BUYING AND SHORTING CANDIDATES WITH THE BEST ODDS OF SUCCESS

Let's briefly sum up what you've learned in this chapter.

Stocks within the same industry group tend to move in the same direction. To take full advantage of this phenomenon:

- ☑ Each day find out what the 5 to 10 strongest and weakest industry groups are.
- ☑ If you want to find breakout setups that have the best odds of launching into monster **up-moves**, look for them in the **strongest industry groups.**
- ☑ If you want to find breakdown setups that have the best odds of launching into monster **down-moves**, look for them in the **weakest industry groups.**
- ☑ Be on the lookout for new emerging industry group leaders (both strong and weak) that move up in the rankings. Monitor these groups for breakout and breakdown candidates that may bear fruit if these groups jump up to the top rankings.

Following industry group leadership and using them to steer you toward the best buying and shorting candidates is an important piece of the puzzle.

In the next chapter I will show how industry group analysis works hand in hand with all the other pieces of the puzzle. Once they are all assembled and you are applying them every single day, you will see the full potential of my trading methodology.

CHAPTER SIX

How To Select Stocks That Consistently Achieve Maximum Gains

With this chapter, you are reaching a major milestone in your journey toward becoming a successful investor. Up until now I have been laying the ground work by teaching you the most important pieces of my Methodology. You have learned how to . . .

. . . **Properly read and interpret a bar chart** (Chapter 2) the way that investment professionals do. Knowing this allows you to . . .

. . . **Identify basic breakouts** (Chapter 3), the patterns that are at the core of my investment strategy. Breakouts are a major component of the strategy that allows you to successfully . . .

. . . **Time the markets** (Chapter 4), the single biggest influence on the movement of any individual stock that you buy. And this goes hand in hand with your . . .

. . . **Focus on stocks within leading industry groups** (Chapter 5) in order to boost the odds of every trade you make.

Now, we'll put all these pieces together so that you can do what every trader and investor on Wall Street wants to do: **SELECT THE RIGHT STOCKS!**

In this chapter, I will provide you with the rules that tightly integrate all of these components with some other key tools into a **single cohesive methodology.**

KALTBAUM'S RULES FOR SUCCESSFULLY BUYING AND SHORTING STOCKS

Note: All of the information that I use in my stock selection process is available from Daily Graphs and Daily Graphs Online. I use both, but if I had to pick only one, it would be Daily Graphs Online because the information is updated every day. Information about how to subscribe to these services is available in the Appendix.

Now, I will walk you through two sets of rules, one for finding stocks that are potentially ready to make a **huge move to the upside** and the other for finding stocks potentially ready to make a **sharp decline.**

Before I do that, let me explain that any stock you consider trading, whether you are looking to buy it or short it, should meet two minimum criteria.

- **The stock must trade with sufficient volume:** You need an average minimum of 250,000 shares traded each day.
- **The stock should be trading at a decent price:** Generally it is best to buy or short stocks that are trading above $12. I do make exceptions, however, from time to time whenever I see a particularly attractive setup.

It is a good idea to limit the majority of your purchases to these preliminary criteria, especially with regard to volume.

OK, let's go through each of my rules. A good way to stay focused is to think the way I'm thinking. As I flip through thousands of stocks in my nightly research, it is almost as though I am possessed by a maniacal obsession.

> **Show me the power! I want the strongest stock in the strongest group with the strongest high-volume breakout. Never settle for the mediocre! Sure, I can find lots of names—but show me the power and I get excited!**

Relative Strength Basics

Relative Strength or RS is an indicator that plays a key role on my buy candidate checklist. For readers who are not familiar with this tool, here is a brief rundown of what it does for you.

RS is a ranking of 1 to 100 that tells you how strong an individual stock is compared to all the other stocks in the market. What this simple indicator allows you to do is isolate strong stocks when the market is weakest and isolate weak stocks when the market is strongest.

When the market is weak and many stocks are getting trashed, I like to see stocks forming bases that simply refuse to go down. These are stocks with RS ranks of 80 or higher. While the rest of the market is going down, these stocks are either zig zagging within their bases, or moving steadily higher within their bases. This is a strong indication that once the market recovers, these stocks will be among those making the most explosive moves higher.

MY RULES FOR SELECTING BUY CANDIDATES

Here is my checklist for finding stocks that will potentially make the most powerful and longest lasting gains to the upside. *Where appropriate, I list the section of this book that you can refer back to if you need to review a concept.*

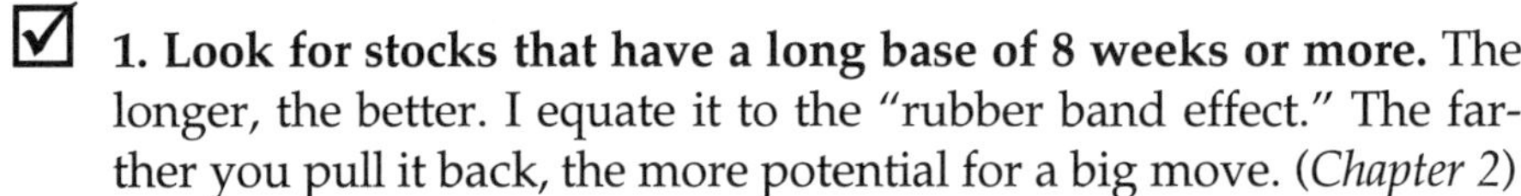

☑ **1. Look for stocks that have a long base of 8 weeks or more.** The longer, the better. I equate it to the "rubber band effect." The farther you pull it back, the more potential for a big move. (*Chapter 2*)

☑ **2. Watch for the stock's price action to tighten for the course of 3 to 7 days as it approaches a potential breakout.** For example, I want to see a stock trade between $30 and $40 and then rush up to the top of the base. I would then want to see it trade between $37 and $40 before breaking out. *Note: While this is what I prefer to see, it doesn't always have to happen. So, if all of the other pieces are in place, I won't be insistent on this one criterion.* (*Chapter 3*)

☑ **3. In a big one-day move, you suddenly see the stock break out on huge volume.** For small- to mid-cap stocks I need to see 2 to 3 times the average daily volume (averaged over the past 30 days). For bigger-cap stocks, 1.5 times the average daily volume will do the trick. The heavy volume indicates that institutions are heavily buying into the stock. That provides fuel for a long, extended rise. (*Chapter 3*)

☑ **4. Make sure that the overall stock market is in a confirmed rally**—Remember the major trend in the overall market is going to have a great influence on the movement of any stock you buy. Make sure that it is moving in your favor and not against you. (*Chapter 4*)

☑ **5. Make sure the stock is in a leading group.** The stock has to be in an industry group that is among the strongest in the entire market. (*Chapter 5*)

☑ **6. Make sure the stock has high relative strength or is rapidly rising in the rankings.** I look for a ranking of 70 or higher, but I am not a stickler about that as long as I see its ranking getting rapidly stronger over the course of 4 weeks or more prior to the breakout. (*See "Relative Strength Basics" on page 95*)

☑ **7. Confirm that "cousin" stocks are making similar moves.** Within stocks of related industries, you want to see the same kind of constructive price-and-volume action that I've described above, i.e., long bases, breakouts on heavy volume, and high relative strength. (*Chapter 5*)

MY RULES FOR SELECTING SHORT-SELLING CANDIDATES

Here are my breakdown criteria for stocks that I would consider shorting. *Note that while there are similarities to the process of looking for stocks to buy, there are major differences. For example, a long base is not required for shorts. So, don't assume that my shorting criteria are simply the opposite of my buying criteria. Also, because of the specialized nature of short-selling, I will expand on some of the checklist items below in Chapter 8.*

☑ **1. Look for the overall market to be headed lower or consolidating.** First and foremost, you need a market that is weak or trading within a range. However, because our stock strategy is to buy stocks that are breaking off a strong uptrend, it should come as no surprise that the overall market itself will often be coming off a strong uptrend. That period of consolidation in which the market is bouncing within a range is fertile ground for shorting opportunities in individual stocks. (*Chapter 4*)

☑ **2. Watch for stocks breaking support on heavy volume.** While the support that is broken can be the lows of a long base, it doesn't have to be. And in fact, it usually isn't. A stock that is going to give you a nice shortable top is usually one that has been in a long uptrend. It's actively pumped by the analysts. They're talking about it on CNBC. It consolidates and forms a bit of support, and then it plummets on heavy volume. (*Chapters 3 and 8*)

☑ **3. After a stock breaks below support, look for it to start rallying up to resistence on light volume after a heavy-volume dip.** One of my favorite tradable setups is where a stock has already broken major support and then it creeps back up to a major moving average, such as the 50-day MA or the 200-day MA, setting up another steep plunge. These two moving averages are widely followed by major institutions. Heavy selling often occurs when a stock breaks below either one of them. (*I will show you this beautiful setup in Chapter 8*)

☑ **4. Make sure the stock is in a weak industry group.** The group that your shorting candidate is part of should be weak and gathering momentum to the downside. (*Chapter 5*)

☑ **5. Confirm that "cousin" stocks are making similar moves.** Look for stocks across related industry groups to be setting up for breakdowns according to the criteria I've mentioned. (*Chapter 5*)

NOW LET'S PUT ALL THIS KNOWLEDGE TO WORK

In the next two chapters, I will show you numerous examples of my methodology at work.

My goal is that with these examples, as well as the practice that you do on your own, you'll be able to flip through hundreds of charts and rapidly identify the potential winners.

Ready? Let's go to Part III.

PART III

Trading Stocks The Gary Kaltbaum Way

CHAPTER SEVEN

How To Buy The Right Stock At Precisely The Right Time

By methodically applying these rules every day, you will have the ability to build and maintain lists of stocks that have the potential to make huge gains. As you study the examples on the following pages and then analyze the markets on your own, keep in mind the following key points:

- **The best breakouts tend to come in big flurries.** The more stocks I see breaking out over the course of several days to several weeks, the more confident I am that the breakouts I participate in are going to produce big moves.

- **The most risky breakouts are the ones that happen apart from other stocks doing the same.** If I see what appears to be a breakout that fits all my criteria, but it's one of a small handful that are occurring, I either stay out of it or buy a small number of shares.

- **Watch for extreme volume days in the market as a whole.** When that happens, it means that there are many stocks getting a huge influx of volume and you should be watching for breakouts like a hawk.

- **Always focus on the industry groups that are leading.** As I have said repeatedly, this is often where you'll find the best buy candidates.

Now let me show you how all of these pieces work together.

Figure 7-1

Reprinted courtesy of Prophet Financial Systems, Inc.—www.prophet.net

In Biovail (BVF), you have all the ducks lined up.

☑ 1. You have a long base that well exceeds the 8-week minimum. Figure 7-1 shows 7 months, but as you'll see in the longer-term view in Figure 7-2, it's actually much longer than that.

☑ 2. There was a tightening of the price action just before the breakout.

☑ 3. Just as BVF broke out, huge volume kicked in.

☑ 4. The market is in a confirmed bull market. In June 1999, the market was in the midst of a powerful rally that began after the 1998 mini-crash.

☑ 5. BVF was in a hot industry group, i.e., second-tier drug manufacturers.

☑ 6. BVF not only had a high RS at the time of the breakout, it had been steadily climbing up the rankings over the course of 6 weeks prior to the breakout day.

☑ 7. Cousin stocks such as Allergan (AGN), Cell Genesys (CEGE), ICOS (ICOS) and Millennium Pharmaceuticals (MLNM) within the same industry group were strong or beginning to break out at the same time as BVF.

And what does all of this mean to you? Turn the page and find out.

Figure 7-2

Reprinted courtesy of Prophet Financial Systems, Inc.—www.prophet.net

BVF shot right to the moon over the next two years, oblivious to the bear market that got everybody uptight beginning in March of 2000. Do they all work out this perfectly? Of course not. Plus, you would not have necessarily had the foresight to have stayed in the stock for the entire duration of the move. But the point I'm making is to stick with the discipline. Do your homework. Make your move. And you'll decide your own destiny.

Let's look at some more.

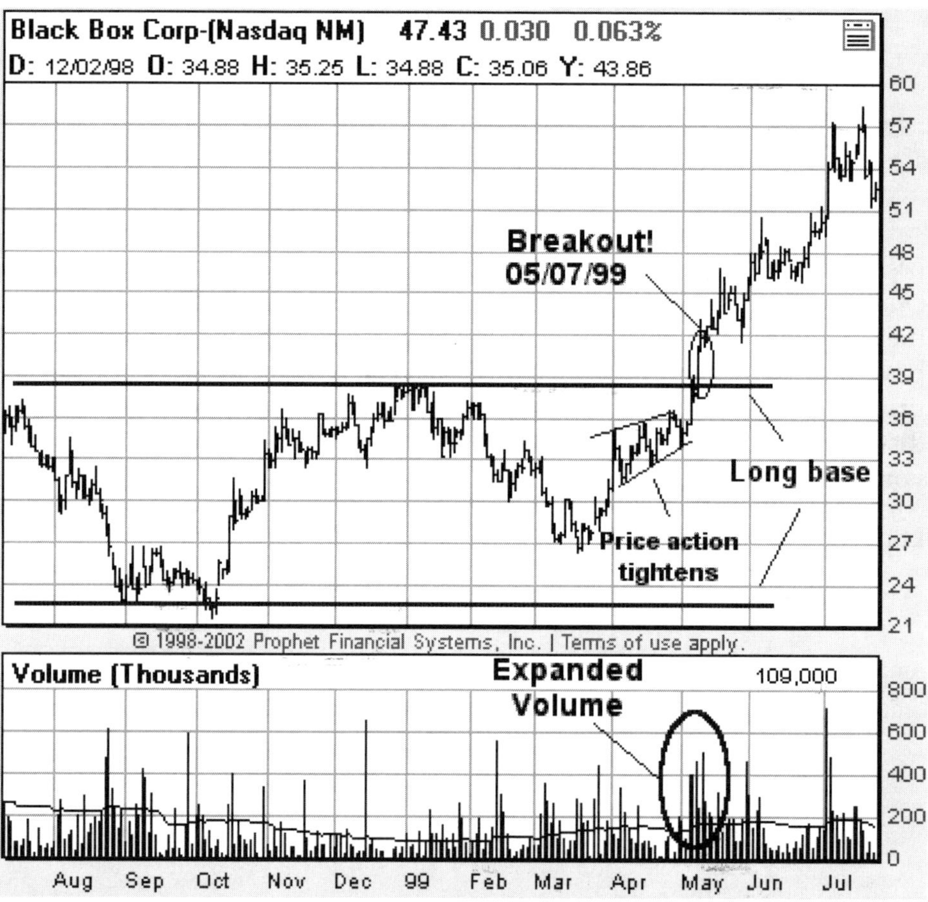

Figure 7-3

Reprinted courtesy of Prophet Financial Systems, Inc.—www.prophet.net

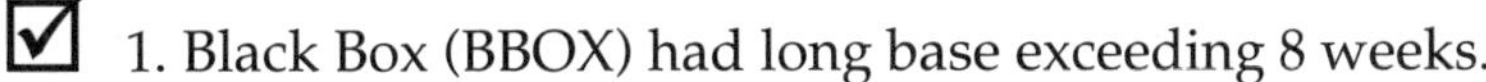

Let's go through the same process:

- ☑ 1. Black Box (BBOX) had long base exceeding 8 weeks.
- ☑ 2. Before the breakout, there was a tightening of the price action.
- ☑ 3. The breakout occurred on huge volume.
- ☑ 4. The market is in a confirmed bull market.
- ☑ 5. BBOX was in the Computer Networking Industry group. That was one of the groups that not only was strong at the time of BBOX's breakout, it also led the market into a wild upward surge later in 1999.
- ☑ 6. BBOX had a high RS and its RS rose for about 6 weeks prior to the breakout.
- ☑ 7. What were BBOX's cousins doing? There were breakouts all over the place. You had names like Adaptec (ADPT), Cisco (CSCO), 3com (COMS), and many others that were exploding at the time.

Let's see how BBOX did.

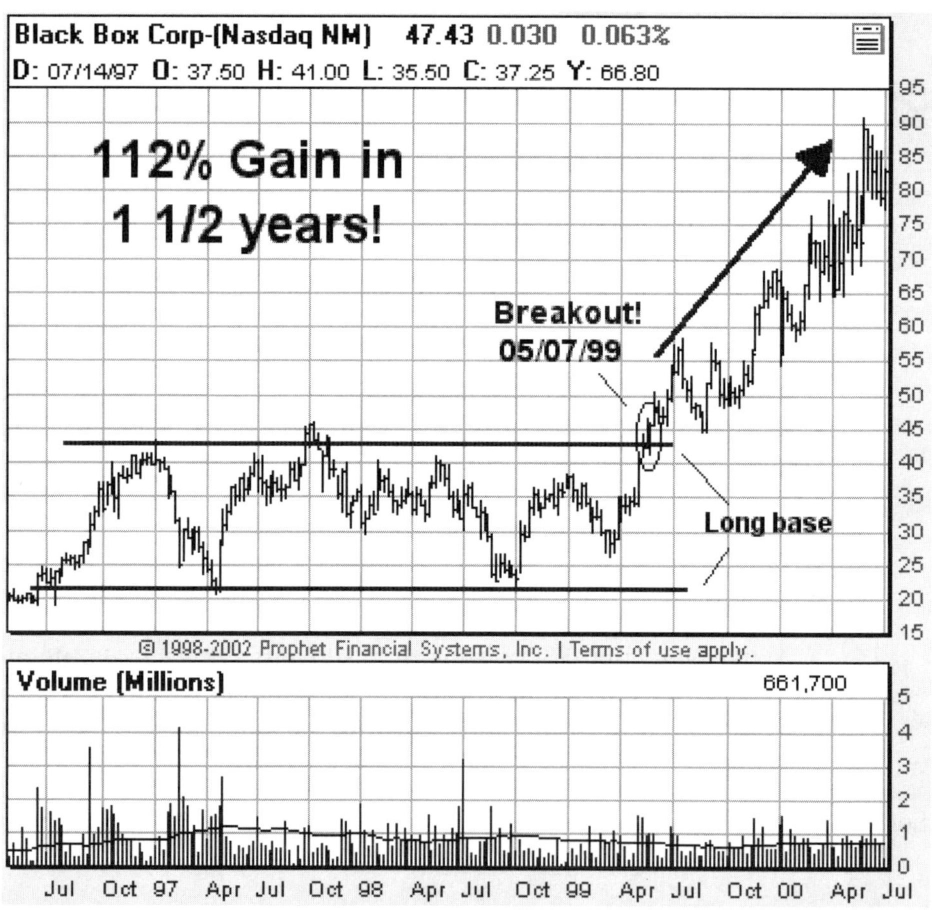

Figure 7-4 Reprinted courtesy of Prophet Financial Systems, Inc.—www.prophet.net

BBOX took off and never looked back. In fact, in a year and a half, it more than doubled. Figure 7-4 shows you the long base from which the stock made this spectacular move. Notice that the base had been forming for two-and-a-half years. That, my friend, is a relatively long time, and it is a setup that I lust after.

> **Remember, the longer the base, the more powerful the breakout and subsequent move is likely to be.**

Next . . .

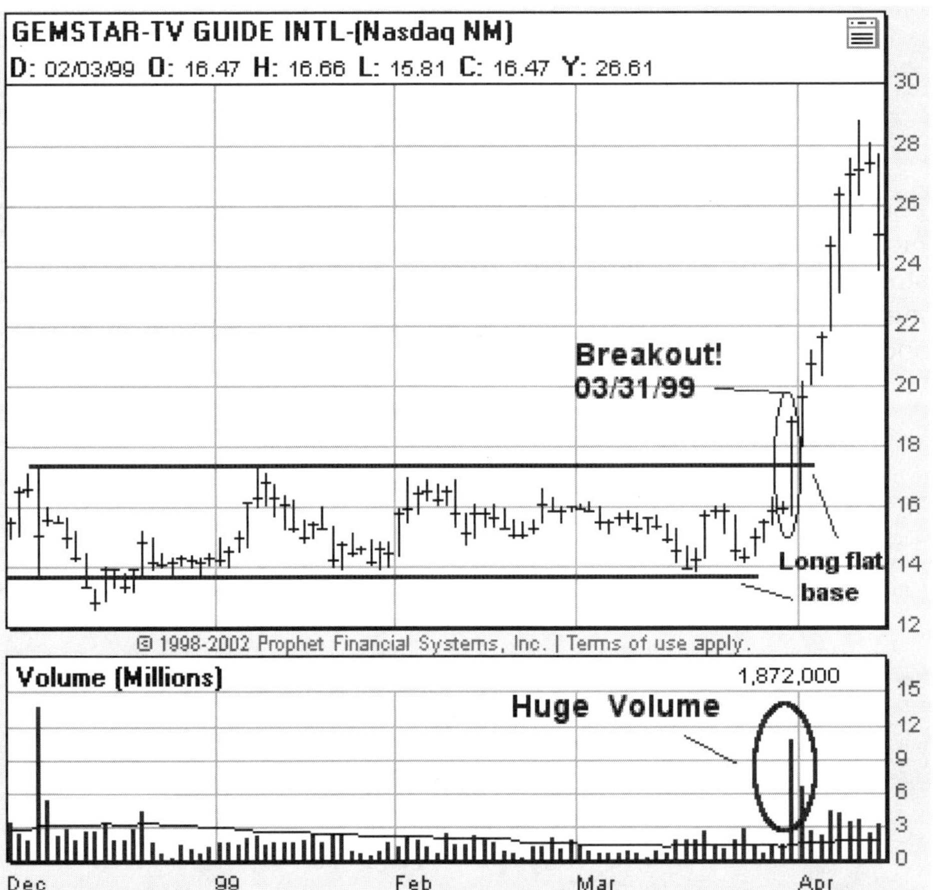

Figure 7-5

Reprinted courtesy of Prophet Financial Systems, Inc.—www.prophet.net

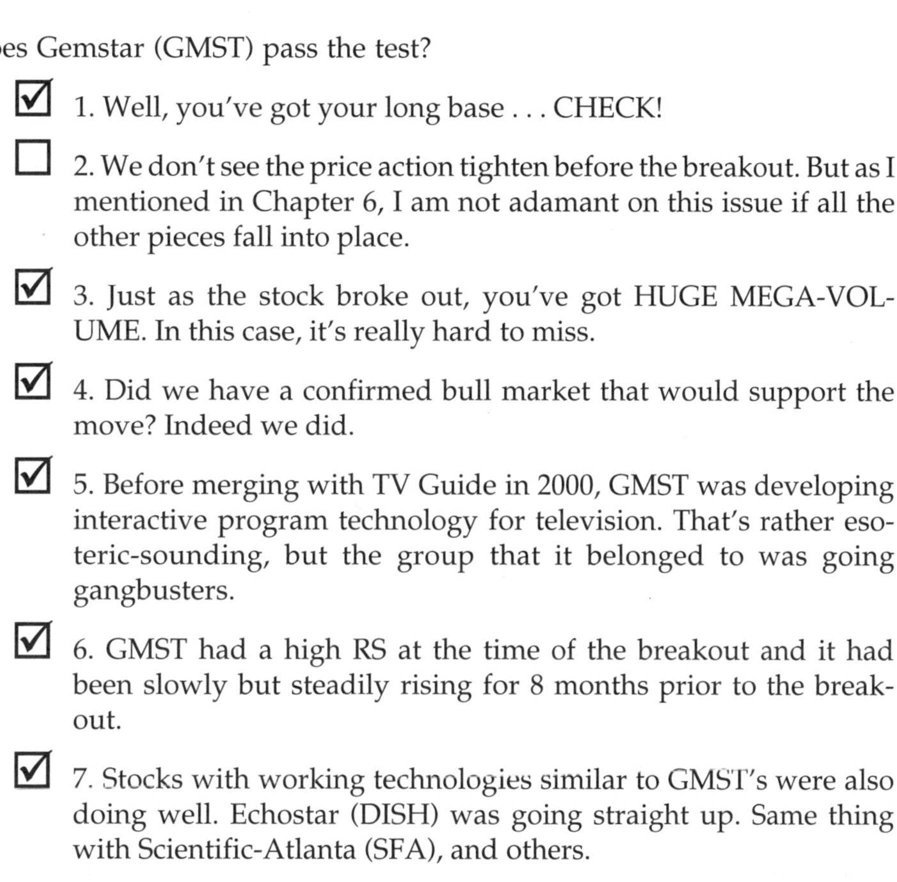

Does Gemstar (GMST) pass the test?

☑ 1. Well, you've got your long base . . . CHECK!

☐ 2. We don't see the price action tighten before the breakout. But as I mentioned in Chapter 6, I am not adamant on this issue if all the other pieces fall into place.

☑ 3. Just as the stock broke out, you've got HUGE MEGA-VOLUME. In this case, it's really hard to miss.

☑ 4. Did we have a confirmed bull market that would support the move? Indeed we did.

☑ 5. Before merging with TV Guide in 2000, GMST was developing interactive program technology for television. That's rather esoteric-sounding, but the group that it belonged to was going gangbusters.

☑ 6. GMST had a high RS at the time of the breakout and it had been slowly but steadily rising for 8 months prior to the breakout.

☑ 7. Stocks with working technologies similar to GMST's were also doing well. Echostar (DISH) was going straight up. Same thing with Scientific-Atlanta (SFA), and others.

Let's see how GMST did.

Figure 7-6

Reprinted courtesy of Prophet Financial Systems, Inc.—www.prophet.net

This example highlights the power of a breakout on heavy volume from a long flat base. It's a picture that has been etched into my memory banks, and I am in a constant search for these stocks. It is no different from a search for an exact piece of real estate or panning for gold . . . except you don't have to leave the comfort of your home to do it.

I strongly suggest that you print out charts like these and tape them to your refrigerator. If you become weary of the Nightly Preparation process, these charts will remind you of the potential rewards of sticking with it.

Next . . .

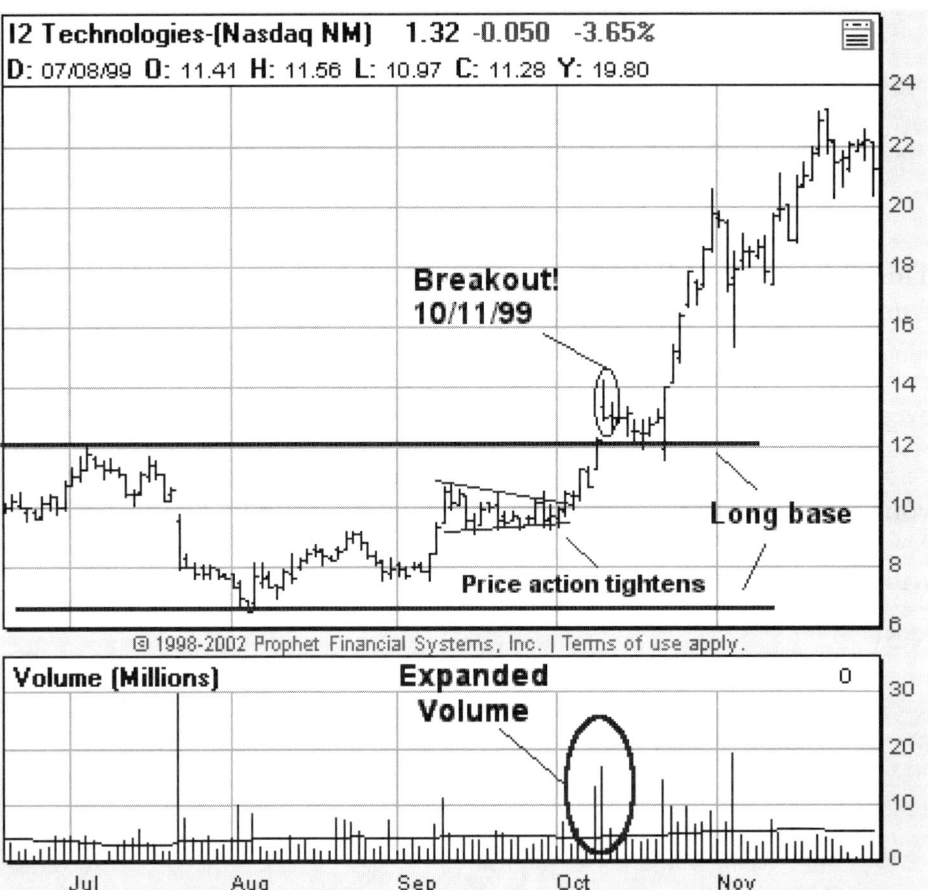

Figure 7-7 Reprinted courtesy of Prophet Financial Systems, Inc.—www.prophet.net

What about I2 Technologies? Are we interested?

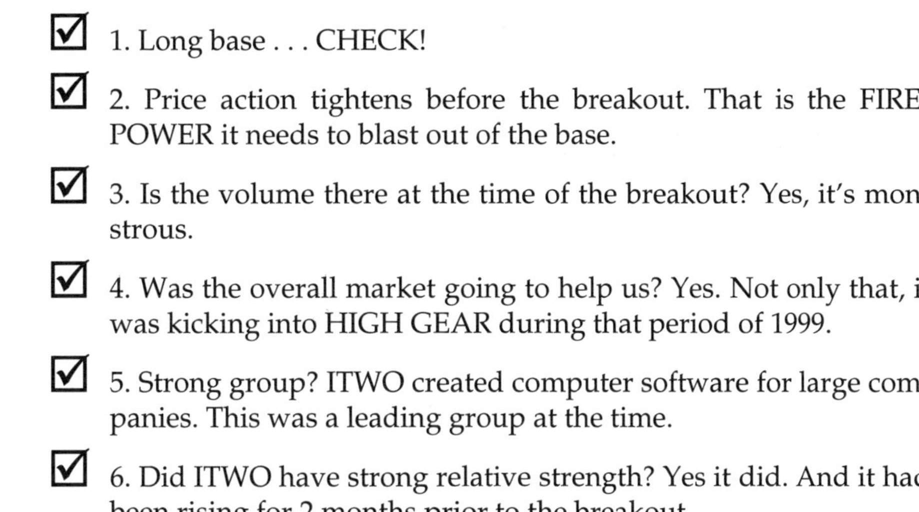

- ☑ 1. Long base . . . CHECK!
- ☑ 2. Price action tightens before the breakout. That is the FIREPOWER it needs to blast out of the base.
- ☑ 3. Is the volume there at the time of the breakout? Yes, it's monstrous.
- ☑ 4. Was the overall market going to help us? Yes. Not only that, it was kicking into HIGH GEAR during that period of 1999.
- ☑ 5. Strong group? ITWO created computer software for large companies. This was a leading group at the time.
- ☑ 6. Did ITWO have strong relative strength? Yes it did. And it had been rising for 2 months prior to the breakout.
- ☑ 7. Cousin stocks were ramping up along with ITWO. You could see similar patterns unfolding in BEA Systems (BEAS), Filenet (FILE), Imation (IMN), and many others.

Can you guess how ITWO did? I bet you can.

Figure 7-8

Reprinted courtesy of Prophet Financial Systems, Inc.—www.prophet.net

ITWO is a good example of a stock that not only had a great-looking chart, but it was part of the psychotic exuberance that was exemplified in the performance of technology stocks. Of course, it was all over in March 2000, and ITWO tanked to ultimately trade below a dollar. But that doesn't matter to you and me because we are in the business of reacting to the here and now, not trying to predict a better and brighter tomorrow.

Go where the action is. And stay there.

Figure 7-9 Reprinted courtesy of Prophet Financial Systems, Inc.—www.prophet.net

Let's go through the exercise, shall we?

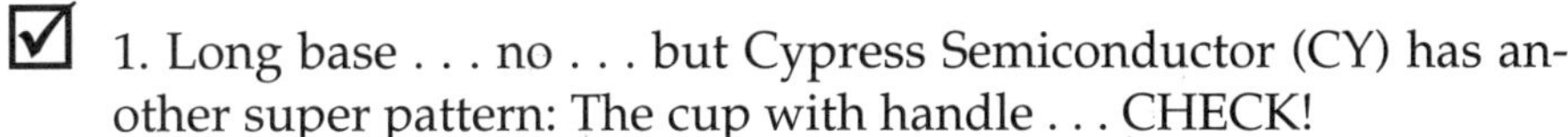

- ☑ 1. Long base . . . no . . . but Cypress Semiconductor (CY) has another super pattern: The cup with handle . . . CHECK!
- ☑ 2. The "handle" of a cup with handle is by nature the tightening of the price action. So, CHECK!
- ☑ 3. Is the volume there at the time of the breakout? YOU BET IT IS!
- ☑ 4. Was the overall market going to help us? Yes!
- ☑ 5. Strong group? Well, any stock that had anything to do with the Semiconductor group had a big edge at that time.
- ☑ 6. Did CY have strong relative strength? Yup. And it had been rising for over 2 months prior to the breakout.
- ☑ 7. Cousin stocks like Intel (INTC), Advanced Micro Devices (AMD), and Texas Instruments (TXN) were *the center of the universe.*

Guess how CY did. I'm sure you're right!

Figure 7-10

Reprinted courtesy of Prophet Financial Systems, Inc.—www.prophet.net

It is very important not to get mesmerized to the point where you stop thinking.

CY is a case where you had the strength of its underlying group, Semiconductors, on the radar screens of institutions, analysts, CNBC and the public investors. That was all the more reason to enjoy the wave while it lasted, but at the same time, be very careful to watch for the signs of a top which we covered in Chapter 6.

While we're on the subject of Semiconductors . . .

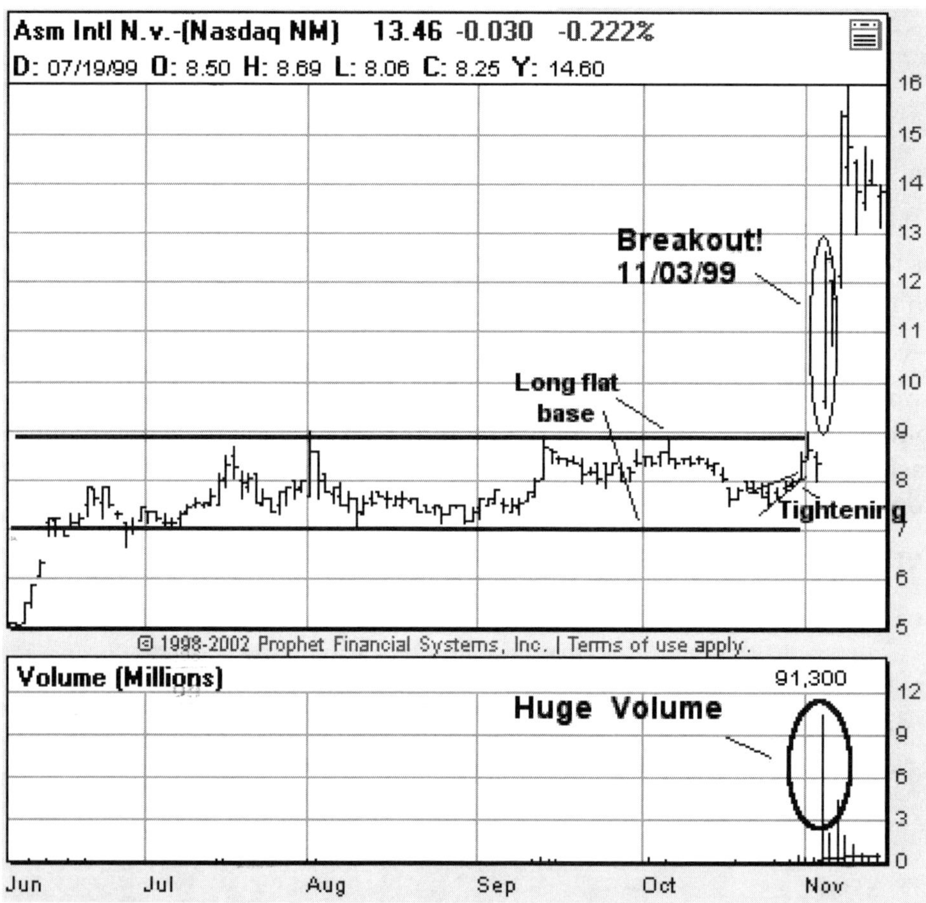

Figure 7-11

Reprinted courtesy of Prophet Financial Systems, Inc.—www.prophet.net

. . . Let me show you another one.

☑ 1. Long base in ASM International (ASMI) . . . yeah . . . can't miss it.

☑ 2. You can see the tightening of price action prior to the explosive move above the trading range.

☑ 3. Volume didn't even seem to exist before the breakout. When the breakout occurs, it's huge!

☑ 4. The market was in one of the highest-velocity rallies in history.

☑ 5. Strong group? Well, ASM provides equipment to the Semiconductor industry, and late 1999 was a good time for the Semis.

☑ 6. Did ASM have strong relative strength? Yes. And it had been rising for 7 months prior to the breakout.

☑ 7. Stocks that were cousins to ASMI, such as Applied Materials (AMAT), Credence Systems (CMOS), Cree (CREE), and others were roaring.

Let's see how it played out.

Figure 7-12

Reprinted courtesy of Prophet Financial Systems, Inc.—www.prophet.net

One thing that is very interesting to know is that ASMI broke out of its base late (11/03/99) in the game, relative to other stocks within or related to the Semiconductor group. For example, CY broke out on 05/07/99. Other Semis broke well before ASMI. When you look at Figures 7-11 and 7-12, what you see is a textbook example of a breakout from a long flat base in a group which already had plenty of advance notice. So, in your Nightly Preparation you would have been especially attuned to stocks with breakout potential within Semis and groups related to Semis. In other words, if you do your job right, ASMI was handed to you on a silver platter.

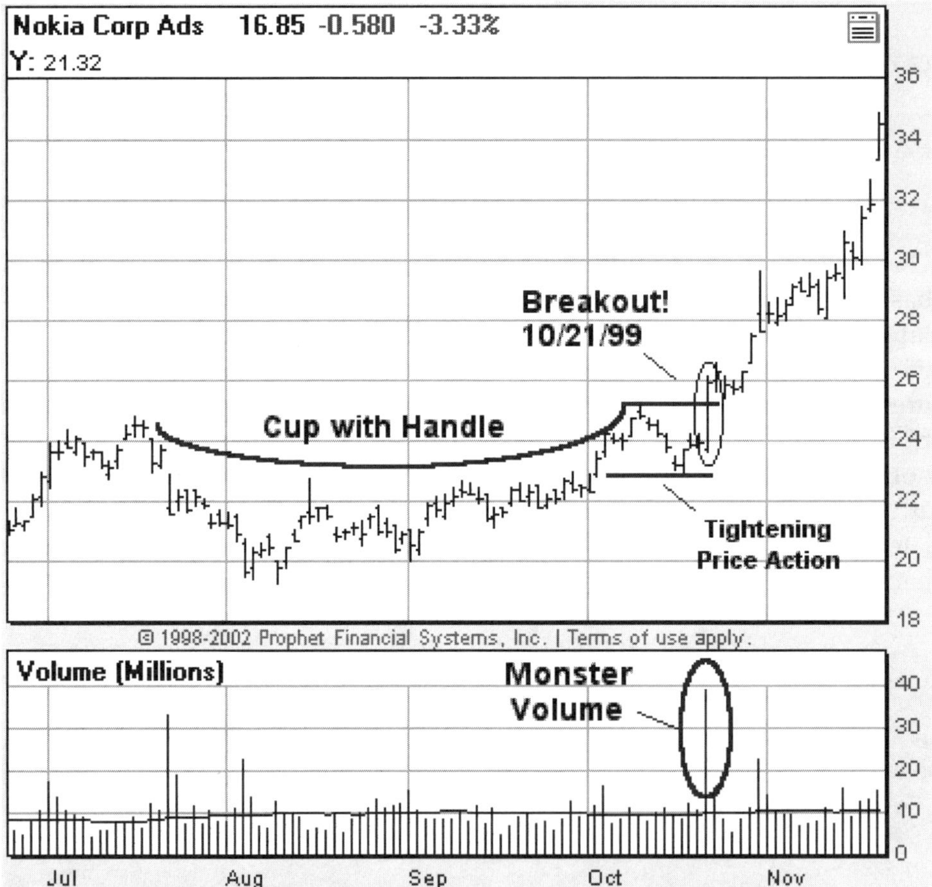

Figure 7-13 Reprinted courtesy of Prophet Financial Systems, Inc.—www.prophet.net

Is this getting to be old hat? I hope so.

- ☑ 1. There was a nice cup with handle in Nokia (NOK) and a breakout from the Handle.
- ☑ 2. As with CY a few examples ago, the Handle is the tightening price action we're looking for.
- ☑ 3. Big volume is there at the time of the breakout.
- ☑ 4. And yes, the market was there to support us with a massive rally.
- ☑ 5. Strong group? Yes, the Telecommunication group was swept up along with technology in general.
- ☑ 6. Did NOK have strong relative strength? Yes, and it had been rising for 2 months steadily prior to the breakout.
- ☑ 7. Cousins were all surging higher. The names included Ericsson (ERICY), Qualcomm (QCOM), Motorola (MOT), and others.

With all the pieces of the puzzle fitting together, what do you suppose happened?

Figure 7-14

Reprinted courtesy of Prophet Financial Systems, Inc.—www.prophet.net

That's a nice move in NOK isn't it?

The beauty of my methodology is that the ability to put on trades like NOK and the others in this chapter is not dependant upon whether we are in a bull or bear market. Many traders and investors learned the hard way with the onset of the bear market in 2000 that those who don't adapt to the market get steam-rollered.

My methodology automatically adapts to whatever the market conditions are. If there are no breakouts . . . guess what? There is nothing for me to get into. And solid breakouts typically occur only when the market is strongly rallying or in the midst of a strong bull market. Do you see what I'm getting at? THIS STRATEGY DOES WHATEVER THE MARKET TELLS IT TO DO.

Figure 7-15 Reprinted courtesy of Prophet Financial Systems, Inc.—www.prophet.net

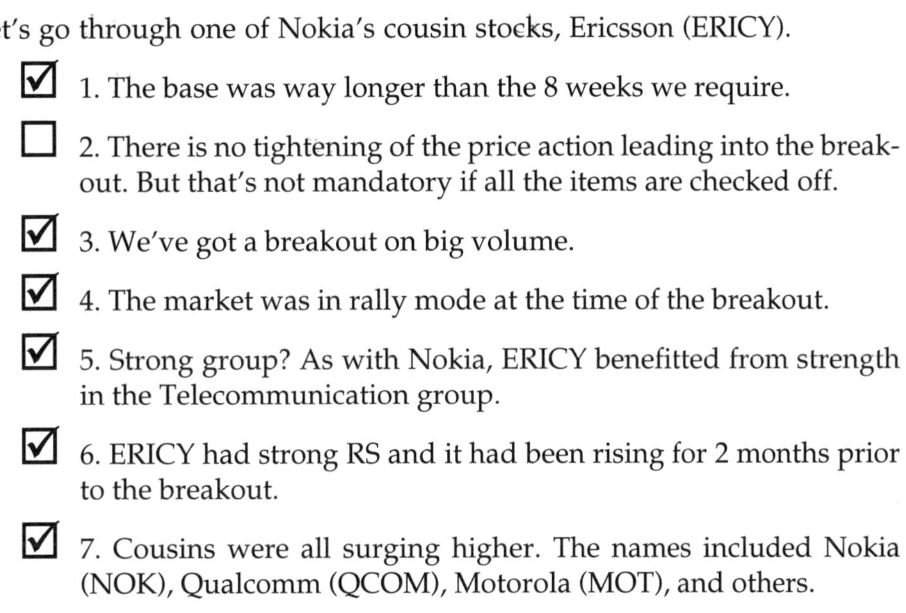

Let's go through one of Nokia's cousin stocks, Ericsson (ERICY).

- ☑ 1. The base was way longer than the 8 weeks we require.
- ☐ 2. There is no tightening of the price action leading into the breakout. But that's not mandatory if all the items are checked off.
- ☑ 3. We've got a breakout on big volume.
- ☑ 4. The market was in rally mode at the time of the breakout.
- ☑ 5. Strong group? As with Nokia, ERICY benefitted from strength in the Telecommunication group.
- ☑ 6. ERICY had strong RS and it had been rising for 2 months prior to the breakout.
- ☑ 7. Cousins were all surging higher. The names included Nokia (NOK), Qualcomm (QCOM), Motorola (MOT), and others.

Let's check out what happened.

Figure 7-16

Reprinted courtesy of Prophet Financial Systems, Inc.—www.prophet.net

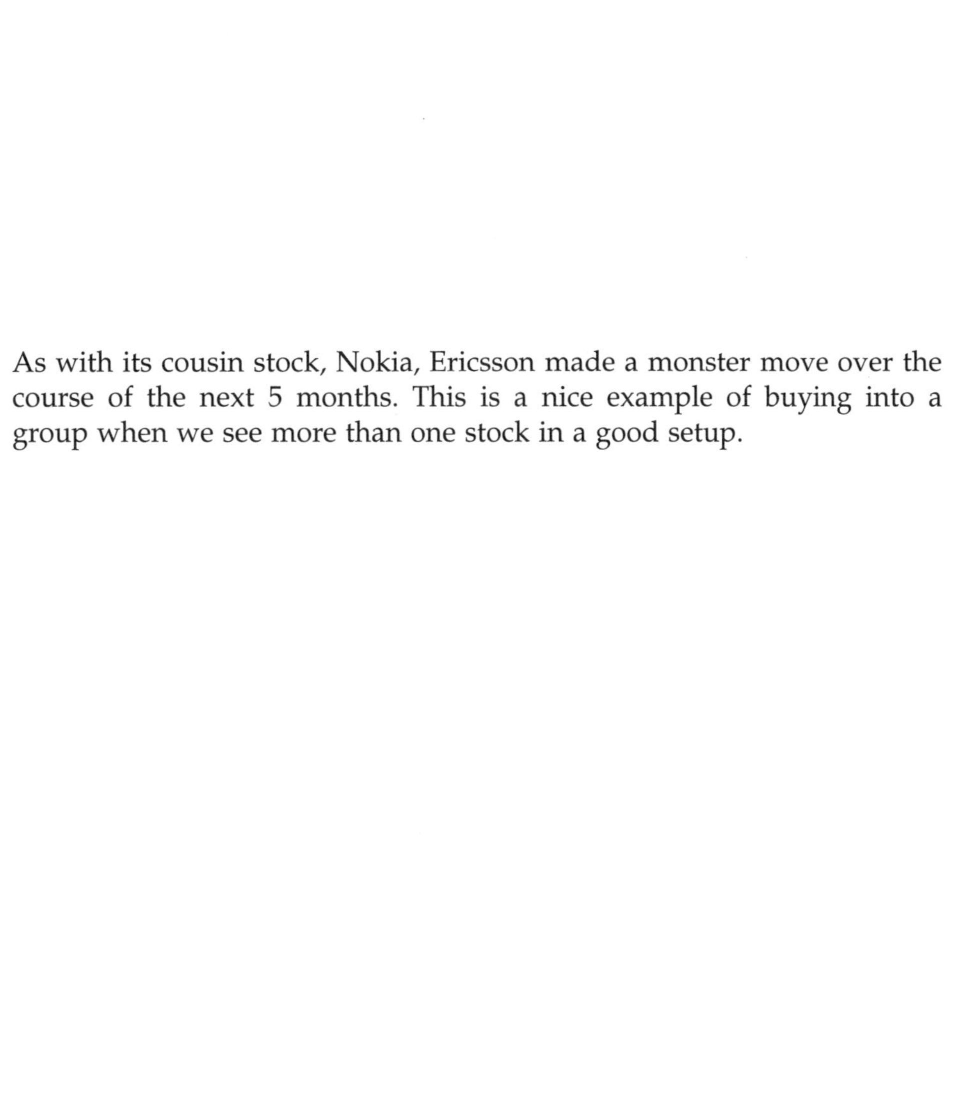

As with its cousin stock, Nokia, Ericsson made a monster move over the course of the next 5 months. This is a nice example of buying into a group when we see more than one stock in a good setup.

Figure 7-17

Reprinted courtesy of Prophet Financial Systems, Inc.—www.prophet.net

Here is one that developed during 2003 and then broke out in early 2004:

- ☑ 1. In CME we see a nice cup with handle play out over the course of 5 months, well in excess of the required 8 weeks.
- ☑ 2. Not only do we get the formation of a handle, the volume dries up as CME drifts lower. This is constructive because it suggestions that institutions are holding onto the stock.
- ☑ 3. Volume explodes on the day of the breakout.
- ☑ 4. On the date of the breakout, the overall market was in a midst of a strong uptrend.
- ☑ 5. CME's industry group, the Securities Brokers, is soaring with the rest of the market.
- ☑ 6. CME had steadily rising relative strength versus the rest of the market.
- ☑ 7. Other stocks in CME's industry were also doing well at the time.

Let's see what kind of action followed the breakout.

Figure 7-18

Reprinted courtesy of Prophet Financial Systems, Inc.—www.prophet.net

CME makes a classic textbook move out of its cup with handle. At the time of this writing, the stock is still in play. That means that if you had entered on the breakout day, you would still potentially be in the stock on the day of the most recent bar shown in the bar chart.

And if you are wondering about how robust my trading methodology is, please note that this trade took place in early 2004. Going back through the many examples I show you throughout this book, you'll see how it is able to operate in a wide diversity of market environments ranging from the 1990s bull market, to the turmoil of the 2000 bear market to the recovery phase that began early 2003.

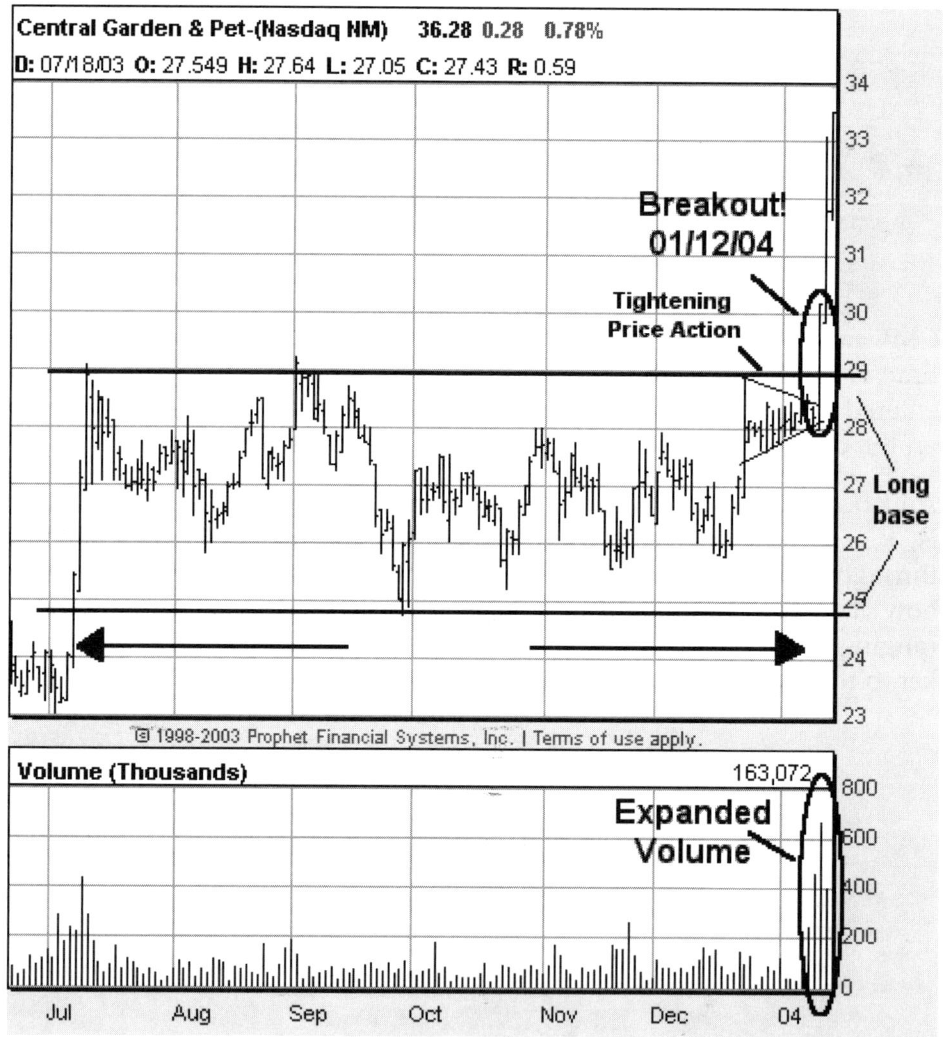

Figure 7-19

Reprinted courtesy of Prophet Financial Systems, Inc.—www.prophet.net

Here is a basing setup in CENT that quietly formed during 2003 and then came to life in 2004:

☑ 1. The base forms from July 2003 to December 2003, so it easily meets our 8-week minimum.

☑ 2. Just prior to the breakout, the price action tightens up, forming a handle.

☑ 3. On the day of the breakout, the volume soars.

☑ 4. The overall market is in a confirmed uptrend.

☑ 5. CENT's industry group, the Household Products group, is trending higher with the rest of the market.

☑ 6. CENT's relative strength is rising.

☑ 7. Other stocks in the same group as CENT, such as URT, ROV, and CHD are also displaying strength.

Here's what immediately followed that breakout:

Figure 7-20

Reprinted courtesy of Prophet Financial Systems, Inc.—www.prophet.net

As you can see by the volume and price action, interest in CENT perked up in a big way. But because you had been watching the base forming for several months prior to the breakout, it should not have caught you by surprise.

Here's the lesson in all of this. Anybody can recognize a breakout after the fact. But the window of opportunity is very small because much of the gain is made in the first few days after a stock explodes out of a base. Someone who sees a stock for the first time when it breaks out is less likely to react quickly enough than someone who has been calmly stalking the stock for several weeks to several months. I want you to be one of the latter.

Figure 7-21 Reprinted courtesy of Prophet Financial Systems, Inc.—www.prophet.net

Here is an example from mid-2003. I show this to you because this stock showed up on my radar screen well before the subsequent recovery phase in the market was universally accepted as "real."

- ☑ 1. A 4-month base forms.
- ☐ 2. Before the breakout occurs, there is no detectable tightening in the price action. But as mentioned before, that is not an absolute requirement.
- ☑ 3. The stock breaks out with a gap on huge volume.
- ☑ 4. The overall market is in an uptrend.
- ☑ 5. The apparel group that CHS belongs to had been moving higher.
- ☑ 6. Relative Strength is moving higher.
- ☑ 7. Cousin stocks in CHS's industry group, such as CLE, JWN, and LTD were all behaving similarly.

Here's the outcome:

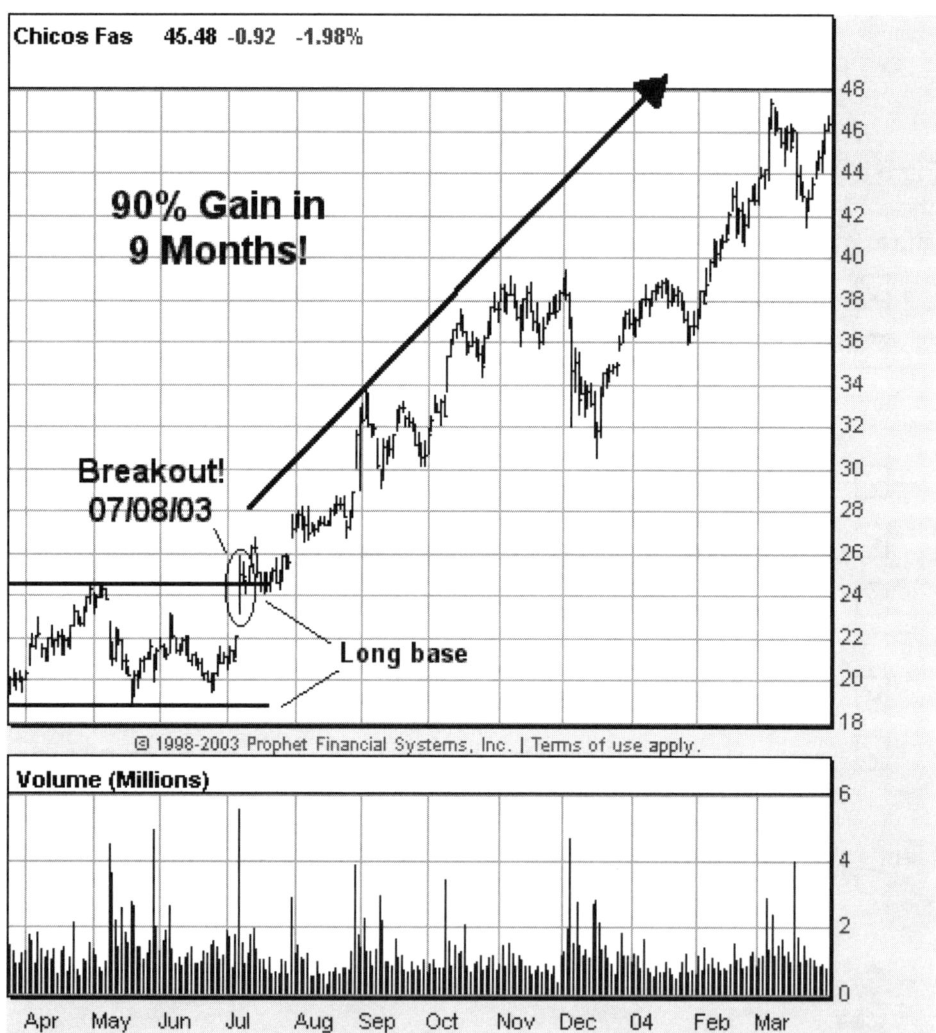

Figure 7-22 Reprinted courtesy of Prophet Financial Systems, Inc.—www.prophet.net

One of the reasons I trade the way I do, is that it allows me to take action without playing guessing games. At times, when the rest of the world is fixated on whether we're in a bear or bull market, I am content with the fact that we're in a "market." The rules I've taught keep me focused on today's market's technical conditions.

CHS in 2003 is a great example of this. At that time, I didn't know whether a new bull market was at hand. Neither did anybody else, but at least I was honest enough to admit it. Yet, there were many opportunities like this one that passed a test containing just 7 simple rules.

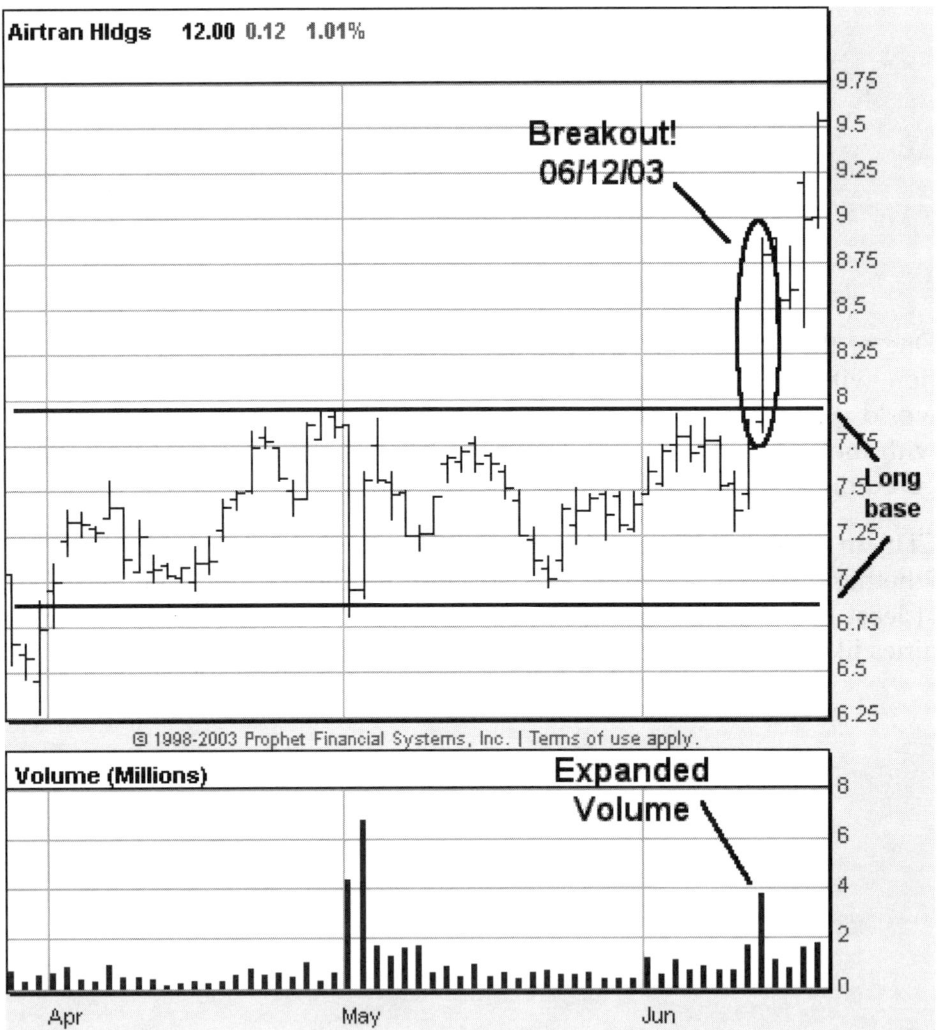

Figure 7-23

Reprinted courtesy of Prophet Financial Systems, Inc.—www.prophet.net

More of the same . . .

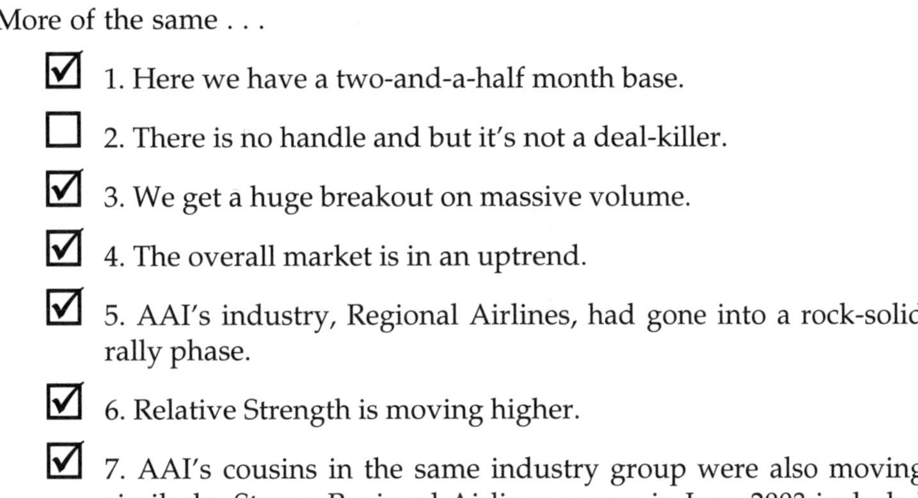

☑ 1. Here we have a two-and-a-half month base.

☐ 2. There is no handle and but it's not a deal-killer.

☑ 3. We get a huge breakout on massive volume.

☑ 4. The overall market is in an uptrend.

☑ 5. AAI's industry, Regional Airlines, had gone into a rock-solid rally phase.

☑ 6. Relative Strength is moving higher.

☑ 7. AAI's cousins in the same industry group were also moving similarly. Strong Regional Airlines names in June 2003 included ALK, AWA, JBLU and LUV.

What do you suppose happened next?

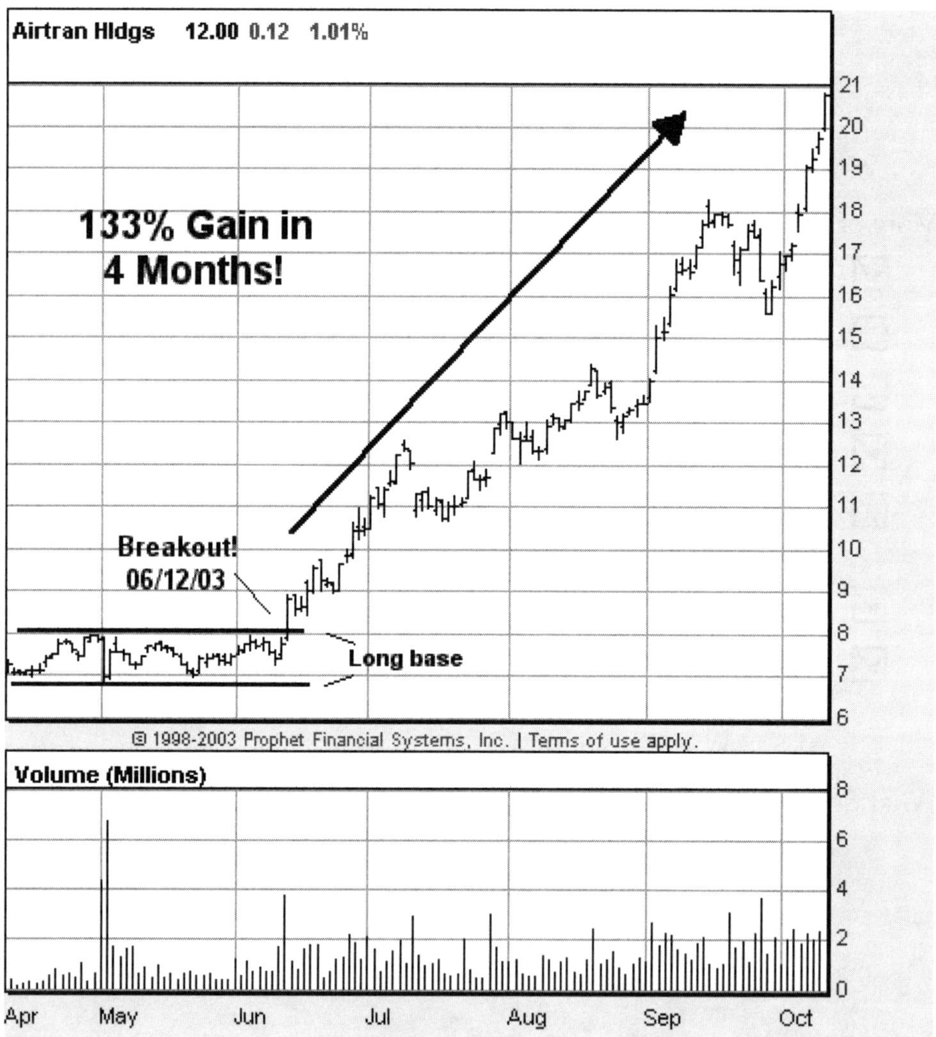

Figure 7-24 Reprinted courtesy of Prophet Financial Systems, Inc.—www.prophet.net

AAI took off and made gains in manner reminiscent of the bull market heyday. Of course, the environment in 2003 did not resemble the reckless abandon that you saw from 1998 to 1999 because many people had the experience of getting burned and losing money. So I would imagine that when stocks like AAI began to move in the way they did, people reacted pessimistically. A great deal of one's success applying the knowledge in this book depends on discipline. We'll be covering that in a later chapter.

At this point you might ask, "Well, Gary, what happens if the market is going down and you see a lot of breakdowns?"

Good question. In Chapter 8, I will show you a powerful way to play the short side of the market.

CHAPTER EIGHT

How To Make Money When Stocks Drop

The general principles that apply to successfully buying stocks are the same when you sell them short. You are looking for stocks to break down below support levels on heavy volume with the market and relevant industry also breaking down.

However, the chart pattern I am going to teach you to find the best short candidates is different and a little more complicated than the one we use for buying. To ensure that you grasp the concepts I will teach you in this chapter, I'm going to review the rules for shorting before I walk you through the pattern.

First let's review some of the mechanics of shorting, if you are unfamiliar with them.

> On a short-sale, you are attempting to profit from the decline in a stock by selling it at a particular price and then buying it back at a lower price . . . pocketing the difference. This is made

possible by your broker who is able to borrow the stock on your behalf from someone else.

The one thing you must keep in mind when short-selling is the uptick rule. This rule, established by the Securities and Exchange Commission, states that you can only short on an uptick, or when a trade is executed at a higher price. With shorts that are executed on a pullback and not a breakout, the effect of the uptick rule is usually negligible. But still, you should always use a limit order when shorting.

Here's what you need in order to find stocks that are potentially going to make a huge move downwards:

☑ **1. Look for the overall market to be headed lower or consolidating.** First and foremost, you need a market that is weak or trading within a range. However, because our stock strategy is to buy stocks that are breaking off a strong uptrend, it should come as no surprise that the overall market itself will often be coming off a strong uptrend. That period of consolidation in which the market is bouncing within a range is fertile ground for shorting opportunities in individual stocks.

☑ **2. Watch for stocks breaking support on heavy volume.** While the support that is broken can be the lows of a long base, it doesn't have to be. And in fact, it usually isn't. A stock that is going to give you a nice shortable top is usually one that has been in a long uptrend. It consolidates and forms a bit of support, and then it plummets on heavy volume.

☑ **3. After a stock breaks below support, look for it to rally up to resistance on light volume after a heavy-volume dip.** One of my favorite tradable setups is where a stock has already broken major support and then it creeps back up to a major moving average, such as the 50-day MA or the 200-day MA, setting up another steep plunge. These two moving averages are widely followed by major institutions. Heavy selling often occurs when a stock breaks below either one of them.

☑ **4. Make sure the stock is in a weak industry group.** The group that your shorting candidate is part of should be weak and gathering momentum to the downside.

☑ **5. Confirm that "cousin" stocks are making similar moves.** Look for stocks across related industry groups to be setting up for breakdowns according to the criteria I've mentioned.

THE CLEAREST AND MOST RELIABLE PATTERN I'VE FOUND FOR PINPOINTING SHORTING OPPORTUNITIES

In the previous chapter I showed you a pattern for identifying great buying opportunities that, under the right circumstances, produce triple-digit returns. When you look at these charts enough times, you can be like a machine finding these breakouts on heavy volume from long flat bases.

Now . . . wouldn't it be great if you could have a pattern that is easy to learn and apply for profiting from stocks that are *going down?* Well, it's contained in item #3 on the previous page: "Rallying up to resistance on light volume after a heavy volume dip."

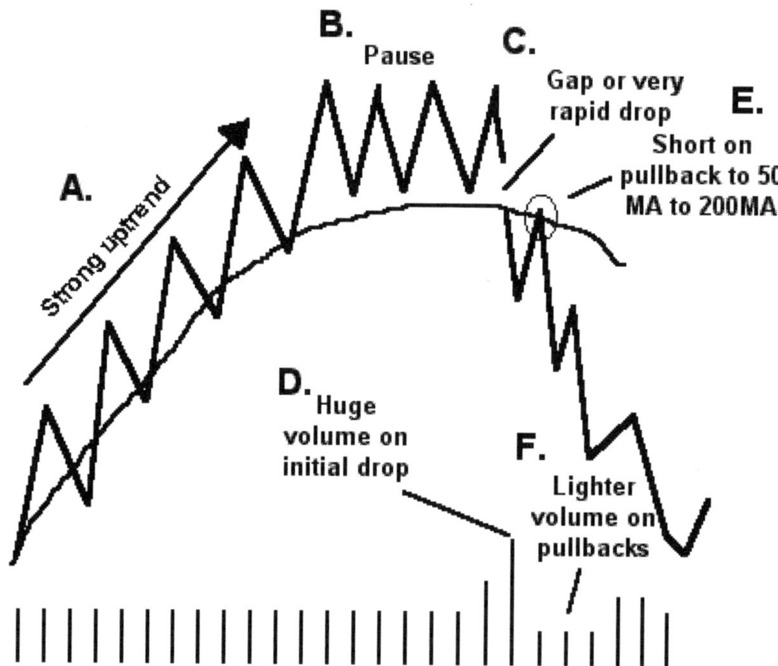

Figure 8-1

It's a little more complicated than the one we use for buying stocks, so I will show it to you in schematic form before we get to the examples. These setups occur when:

A. A stock has had a major runup. You have an extended, seemingly bulletproof uptrend.

B. As the stock seems to be merely pausing prior to a resumption of the uptrend . . .

C. It suddenly and rapidly breaks down on a gap or wide-range day . . .

D. . . . On heavy volume.

E. It pulls back to or near either the 50-day moving average or the 200-day moving average . . .

F. . . . On lighter volume.

Once the stock fails to break above the moving average, that's when the shorting opportunity comes.

Now let me tell you what this pattern does and does not do.

- This is a pattern designed to find *major tops,* and it does not occur very often. But if you do your Nightly Preparation and scan through hundreds to thousands of stocks like I do, you'll find plenty of these setups over the course of a typical year.
- This pattern works most consistently in *packs.* My confidence is at a peak when I see these patterns occur in a great number of stocks within a particular sector or industry group.
- Not all stocks make their final tops according to this pattern, but I focus on this pattern because it provides one of the *clearest and most unambiguous* indications that a stock is about to drop.
- This pattern can be used as your exit strategy for longs.

OK, now let me show you how this pattern works within the grand scheme of my rules for finding good short-sale candidates.

Figure 8-2 Reprinted courtesy of Prophet Financial Systems, Inc.—www.prophet.net

Observe our shorting rules in action:

- ☑ 1. The overall market was consolidating. In the first four months of 1999, the market was chopping around in a range after a huge run-up from the 1998 Russian bank crisis mini-crash. Hindsight tells us, "Hey, you must have been nuts to be shorting because the market was about to explode higher." But remember at that time nobody knew this. You must only trade what you see, and at that time the only thing you saw was the market consolidating. That's good enough to warrant a short on a stock that met the qualifications.
- ☑ 2. We had a breakdown on heavy volume. Eli Lilly (LLY) had a long run up during the course of 1998 and it suddenly gapped lower on heavy volume. Picture perfect.
- ☑ 3. LLY pulled back up to the 50-MA. Following the gap down on heavy volume, LLY rallied back up to the 50-day MA on lighter volume. Further selling was initiated and from there it plunged. This pullback to the 50-day MA is where the shorting opportunity for us comes.
- ☑ 4. LLY's industry group was weak. 1999 was to become a horrible year for the major drug companies. The downtrend for the industry group began early in the year and did not let up until early 2000.
- ☑ 5. LLY's cousins were weak. Stocks like Abbott Labs (ABT), Schering-Plough (SGP), Pfizer and others, were breaking down at the same time.

With all of these pieces coming together, what do you think LLY did? Check it out.

Figure 8-3 Reprinted courtesy of Prophet Financial Systems, Inc.—www.prophet.net

LLY sold off nicely and ultimately broke below its 200-day moving average which triggered even more selling, and for alert traders, another shorting opportunity. This is a great example of the power of industry group analysis. Many major drug stocks shrugged off the strength in the overall market for much of 1999 and either went sideways or headed lower. You must continually look for obvious themes to develop within industry groups and balance that with what you see every day occurring in the major market averages.

Want to see more? Here's another nice example.

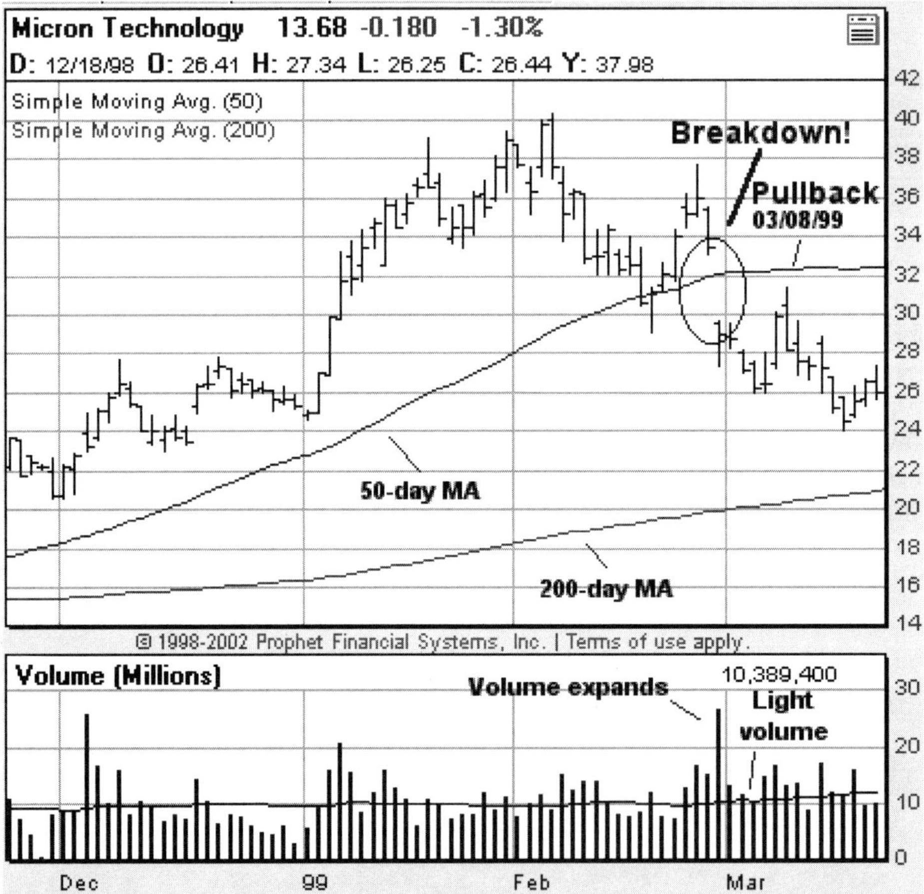

Figure 8-4

Reprinted courtesy of Prophet Financial Systems, Inc.—www.prophet.net

All the ingredients are in place:

- ☑ 1. The market was consolidating in early 1999.
- ☑ 2. In late February, Micron Technology (MU) abruptly gapped down on heavy volume. Gaps like these are great because they are a clear sign that big institutional players are starting to throw in the towel. Once a stock loses support from the big guys, it can change the whole psychology of a stock overnight. Fear takes hold quickly and more selling is triggered.
- ☑ 3. MU pulled back close to the 50-day MA and then reversed suddenly to make lower lows. This failure to even touch the 50-day MA revealed that MU was definitely on the sick list.
- ☑ 4. MU's industry group, memory chips, were weak throughout the first half of the year.
- ☑ 5. You could see weakness in MU's cousins. Among them were: Rambus (RMBS), MIPS Technologies, and others.

Check, check, check, check and check. All the ingredients of a stock ready to crumble. It doesn't always do it, but the odds are in your favor. Here's the action.

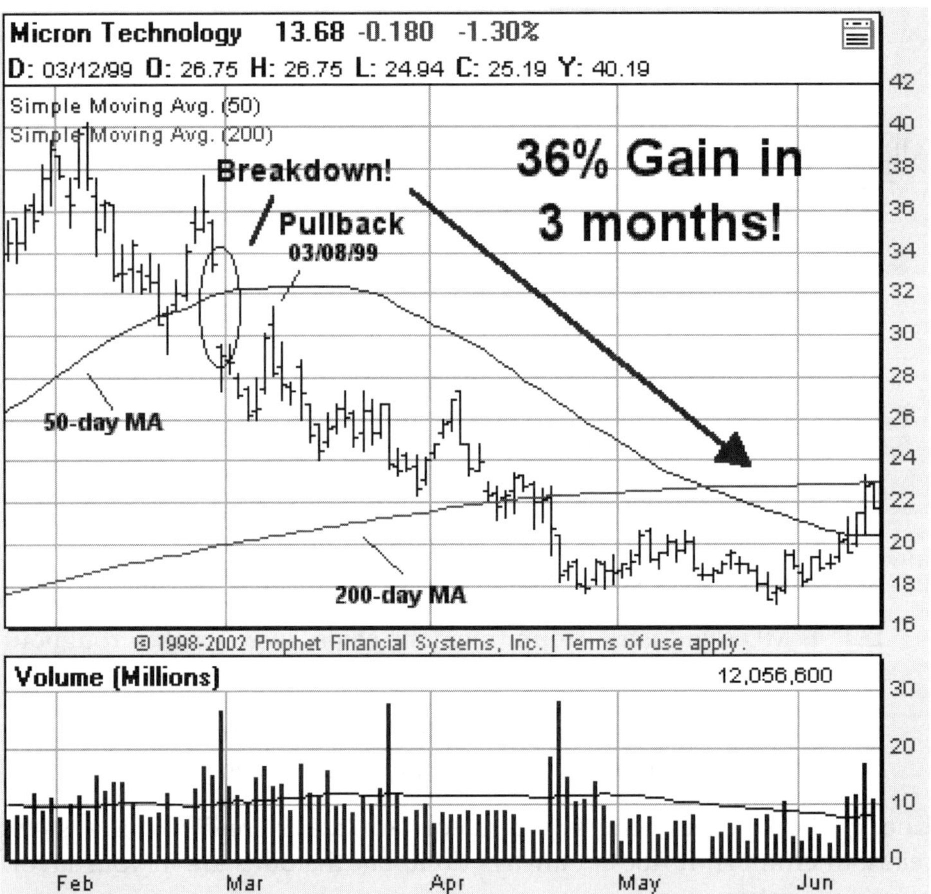

Figure 8-5 Reprinted courtesy of Prophet Financial Systems, Inc.—www.prophet.net

Being able to take a mechanical approach to my shorting strategy is especially important because the stocks I short are often coming off of extended rallies. Unless you have seen it happen as many times as I have, you're liable to get psyched out of taking action on the short side. But keep in mind that a gap down on heavy volume typically causes heavy technical damage to a stock. Can you think of anyone who would buy a stock exhibiting the behavior you see in MU in early March 1999? Probably not. Not only are they not buying, this type of action shakes the confidence of those who hold the stock. Selling leads to even more selling.

You can see this across a wide variety of stocks within different groups. Let's look at another example.

Figure 8-6 Reprinted courtesy of Prophet Financial Systems, Inc.—www.prophet.net

So, what can you say about Gap (GPS) Inc.?

- ☑ 1. During March and April 2000 we had, for all the world to see, a market that was tanking and taking many industry groups down with it.
- ☑ 2. GPS took a nosedive, making a huge gap down below its 50-day MA on massive volume.
- ☑ 3. Only three days later on 04/10/02, GPS was revisiting the 50-day MA for one last time on light volume. It doesn't hang around for very long and just collapses from there.
- ☑ 4. GPS's group, Retail Apparel Stores, had a weak showing in 2000 which paralleled the rest of the market.
- ☑ 5. Other weak cousins included: Nordstrom (JWN), Limited Brands (LTD), Ross Stores (ROST), and others.

Did we do OK? Let's review the subsequent action and see.

Figure 8-7 Reprinted courtesy of Prophet Financial Systems, Inc.—www.prophet.net

Once GPS broke the 50-day MA decisively, it immediately attacked the 200-day MA and won. After that, there wasn't much to keep GPS from going even lower. This is a graphic illustration of why my eyes are glued to these major moving averages. As I mentioned previously, many major institutional traders do not want to be in stocks that break these key moving averages. My strategy enables you to exploit their flight to the sidelines.

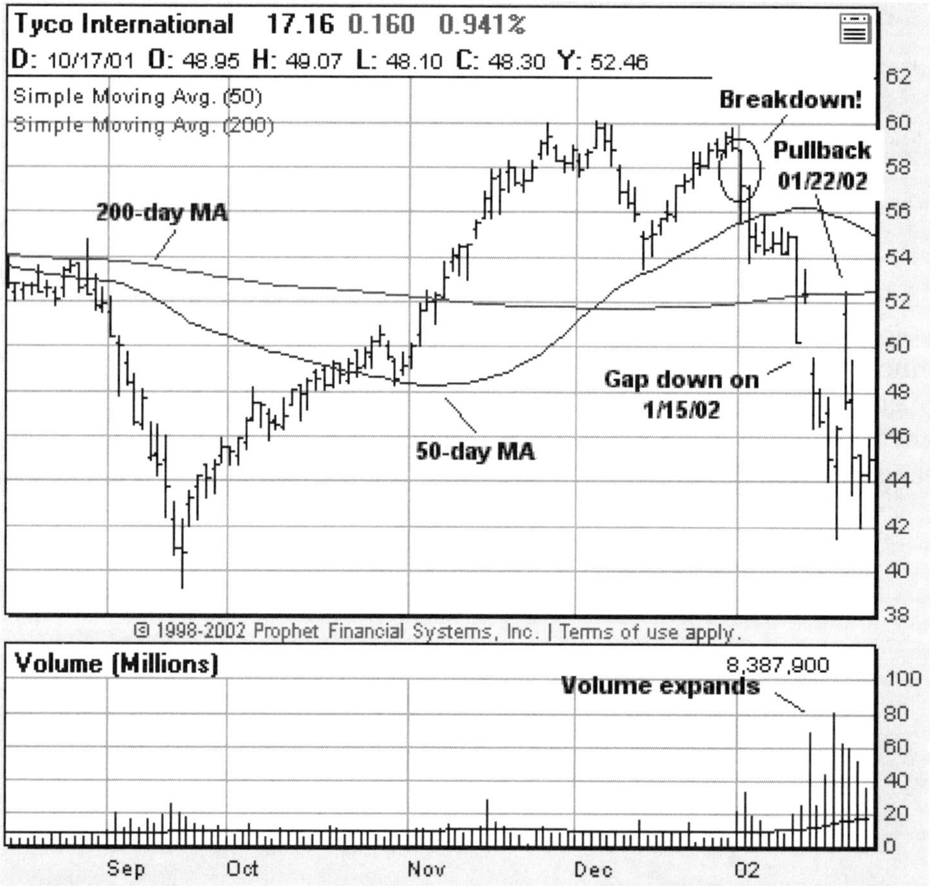

Figure 8-8 Reprinted courtesy of Prophet Financial Systems, Inc.—www.prophet.net

Tyco (TYC) would have to rank as one of my favorite stocks on the short side in 2002.

- ☑ 1. The stock market was accelerating downward for the first half of 2002.
- ☑ 2. TYC fell apart with a monstrous gap on heavy volume, breaking below the key 200-day MA.
- ☑ 3. In a dramatic move, TYC exploded back up to its 200-day MA on 01/22/02. You really don't see the light volume on the pullback because what normally occurs over the course of several days only took one day. Therefore, we can allow for a minor deviation from our strategy. Whatever. This is the mother of all shorting opportunities.
- ☑ 4. The Diversified Operations sector, of which TYC was a component, was weak.
- ☑ 5. Other weak cousins included General Electric (GE), Honeywell (HON), Siemens AG (SI), and others.

TYC was like The Three Stooges heading for the door all at once. Let me explain why.

Figure 8-9 Reprinted courtesy of Prophet Financial Systems, Inc.—www.prophet.net

The stock gapped down on Jan. 15. The gap occurred because the company missed estimates. This was very worrisome for a couple of reasons:

- Tyco reminded me of AOL/Time Warner (AOL). Like AOL, TYC had for months told Wall Street how great things were. And then they miss estimates.

- Combine this miss with the fact that TYC was overowned by institutions and you have a recipe for selling . . . and when they are sold . . . it is like Larry, Moe and Curly crashing into one another on the way to the exit.

Jan. 22, the day TYC bungeed back to its 200-day MA, was the day that put the whammy on the stock. This was the day that Tyco announced the split-up of the company. Yes, those same analysts were out saying that it was a great move for the company . . . that it would unlock tremendous value for all the businesses and that the stock was far undervalued. Well, that was only opinion. The market's opinion was much different. INSTITUTIONS sold into the news . . . and in a big way. How do we know this? On 62 million shares, the stock closed at the lows of the day after being up over $6, closing at $47.55. This was key evidence that the smart money was saying bye-bye to the stock . . . and that is one big freight train that you don't want to get in front of.

The rest is history.

WHY YOU SHOULD LEARN HOW TO SHORT STOCKS

I hope that these examples of my very simple shorting strategy opens your eyes to new possibilities if you have only been a buyer of stocks up to this point. Bear markets can last a long time. If you want some sobering proof of this, take a look at this long-term chart of the S&P 500 Index.

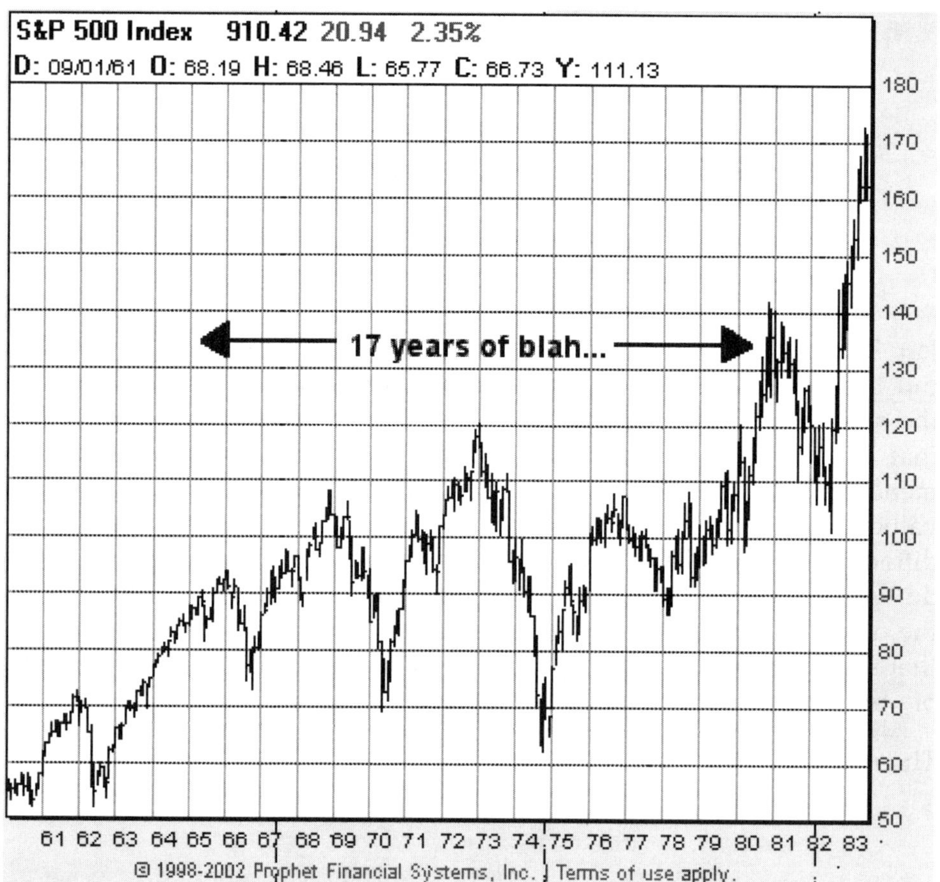

Figure 8-10 Reprinted courtesy of Prophet Financial Systems, Inc.—www.prophet.net

From the mid-'60s to the early '80s, the stock market was a miserable place if you simply held stocks. There were bright spots here and there, but you were generally not getting much of a return.

But I have good news for you. If you learn to play the short side of the market, you won't have to preserve yourself cryogenically so that you can start making money again in the next bull market. The opportunities will continue coming at you in the form of the type of breakdown setups I've been showing you in this chapter.

And always keep this mind: If you look at the stock market over the course of the past 100 years, it always bounced back and exploded to much higher levels. If you are able to wait out the bear markets, the happy times always come back. This has always been the case, and I think it will always play out that way.

We've covered all my main strategies. Now in the next and final chapter, let's remove whatever else remains standing between you and becoming a highly successful investor!

CHAPTER NINE

Planning For A Lifetime Of Profitable Investment Decisions

I have provided you with my best trading knowledge and rules for applying that knowledge. What does it take to *make it all happen* in your life?

In this chapter, making it happen is my focus. Why? Because you can have the best formulas in the world, but without executing them properly, you're just spinning your wheels. I will lay out for you the exact plan that I follow each night (and weekend) in order to ensure that you are able to correctly execute my methodology and consistently nail winning stocks not just today, not just next week, *but for the rest of your life.*

KALTBAUM'S NIGHTLY AND WEEKEND PLAN FOR SUCCESS

If I could give you one word that could describe what it takes to be successful in most any endeavor, let alone finding stocks with quality breakouts that produce long, sustained moves, that word is . . .

PREPARATION!

I am not talking about any old preparing. I am talking about intense meaningful preparation.

You should try not to leave too much to chance. Every day before the market opens, before you go off to work, before you wake the kids up for school, you should have a list of specific stocks to focus on and a firm grasp on which way the market wind is blowing. By achieving this daily mastery of the markets, you accomplish a number of things:

- By being aware of stocks that are just about ready to explode, you will be able to jump into them at the best possible price, should an entry signal occur.

- By having a list of stocks that are in the process of building bases and getting ready to explode at some time in the more distant future, you won't be caught by surprise or wind up chasing them after they have already launched into the stratosphere.

- You will be immune to misleading statements you may hear on the news or opinions expressed by "experts" you meet while riding in a taxi or waiting for an oil change.

- You will not get spooked by every market hiccup, up or down. In other words, all of the indicators I follow, plus the nightly homework I teach you to do, will keep you out of false rallies and help you to buy great stocks when the rest of the world thinks the market is going to hell.

MY PREPARATION RITUAL

My preparation happens on the weekend and every night. I am not just talking about looking at charts. I am talking about getting specific.

Let me give an overview of what I do each day.

Weekends

Starting on Sundays, I take out my *Daily Graphs* (to subscribe, see the resources listed at the end of this book) and spend a minimum of three hours looking for stocks with my specific buy criteria. *Daily Graphs* is a weekly book of stock charts published by William O'Neil and Company which contains specific technical and fundamental criteria that are incorporated into my analysis. Yes, I know there are some chart software programs and websites that allow you to look at a large number of charts. But when I am on my weekly fishing expedition, I prefer using this weekly book because all the information I need is in one place, and there is just something about being able to flip through these things sitting by the pool. I can't do this as well with a laptop.

Those three hours give me a great overall view of the markets. Take note of what the overall market seems to be doing, in accordance with what I taught you in Chapter 4 on Market Timing. Plus, I write down the names of stocks that are of interest according to the checklist that I will provide you with later in this chapter.

Week Nights

First off, let me emphasize that you do not have to build a computer setup that is as elaborate as mine. Remember, the stock market is how I make a living. You can easily accomplish what I do with one inexpensive computer purchased at a Circuit City sale. Now let me tell you what I have: three monitors with thousands of stocks listed. The list is not just in random order. Stocks that are up are in green, stocks that are down are red. I also have the stocks separated by groups. This allows me to quickly see which areas of the market are outperforming or underperforming on any given day. I also have the screens labeled to separate the stage of action certain stocks are in.

That means I have a:

- **Breakout and breakdown page.** These pages contain stocks that are strong candidates for breakouts. These lists are my main source of buy or shorting candidates.
- **Updated new high and new low list.** These lists contains the stocks that are usually the leaders or laggards. By following these stocks, I have a good idea of which direction the leaders or laggards are going to pull the market.
- **Volume page.** This list contains stocks that are up or down on more than average volume. When there is a sudden burst of volume, it indicates that something important may be happening. I look at these charts to see whether any interesting basing patterns are forming. Stocks such as these may already be on my breakout and breakdown page. When they show up here, I have to check to see whether a breakout or breakdown is occurring, and therefore, initiate a buy or short order.
- **Short page.** These are candidates for breakdowns.
- **Setup page.** These are stocks that are ready to buy the next day.
- **TradingMarkets TradersWire.** This is my favorite Internet chat room because it's about the only place I know of where genuinely knowledgeable traders and investors hang out. Of course, this is a daytime pursuit, but I have a screen dedicated to it. You can find out more about how to get a free 7-day trial in the Resources section of this book.

I want to share with you some additional thoughts and insights about the benefits of this Nightly Preparation.

You might think this is all hard work. But is it really? To me, it's more fun than anything else. If you spend hours in front of the TV in order to be entertained, I would ask you the following:

> **What could be more entertaining than spending one hour each night shaping and molding your financial destiny . . . and seeing wealth created right before your very eyes?**

I view this as a simple and methodical process that once you have yourself trained, is automatic. And it can produce nice returns. In fact, many Wall Street professionals are amazed at the gains that the process I've just described can produce. But it's just me in my attic with coffee and a bagel, not a room full of research analysts sitting next to a supercomputer.

HERE'S GREAT NEWS FOR YOUR 401K, RETIREMENT FUNDS, COLLEGE FUNDS, AND LONG-TERM INVESTMENTS

Here's another important benefit of doing this Nightly/Weekend preparation: You will have a moment-by-moment grasp of where the market will go next that is superior to the majority of what Wall Street analysts know.

I do not make statements like this lightly, but I know from my own experience that as I add and subtract stock names from the long and short lists, I actually get a strong (and accurate) feel for what the market is going to do. It's just the kind of common sense that I had mentioned in the chapter on market timing. Follow this logic:

- I am constantly adding to and subtracting from the lists.
- As the list of stocks poised to break out to the upside expands, *I'm looking for a market that is getting ready to go up.*

- As the list of stocks poised to break downward expands, *I'm looking for a market that will likely head lower.*

When I develop these kinds of biases, I'm not making any prediction because I'm not going to enter any trades until I see the breakouts occur. But do you see how this will help you maximize your longer-term investments? Tell me, how will you invest your 401(k) money today? Or what about the money you're saving for your child's tuition?

With Nightly Preparation, there are intelligent ways of making the correct decisions!

> Here's a case in point. In April 2000, I saw a whole boatload of leading stocks top out according to the breakdown criteria I've just described. I told everyone that listens to my radio show to head for the hills.

MY TEN RULES FOR INVESTMENT SUCCESS

Now that you have learned my methodology, you have a solid basis for taking control of your investments and maximizing your returns. In this final chapter, I want to help you to apply all of this knowledge properly by providing you the key insights, one by one, that have enabled me to survive and thrive during both good market environments and, more importantly, challenging ones. Here they are:

Rule #1: Success in the stock market is all about being fully aware of what you know and what you don't know.

> You probably know me well enough by now to know that I am a no B.S. kind of a guy. I have worked my way through the same kind of misguided shooting-from-the-hip that plagues the majority of investors when they first start out in this business. Over time, I experienced enough pain to change my ways. I don't pretend to know it all, but one thing is for sure . . . I know what I don't know and I fully admit it.

I know it's fashionable to take a stance all the time . . . but I don't believe it is worth it.

I have studied all the great traders and technicians on Wall Street. They don't predict, they evaluate. Predicting does not work. Do you remember the book by Ravi Batra? It was called "The Great Depression of the 1990s." DUH! How about the fabulous book "Dow 100,000"? The first book came out at the bottom and the latter came out at the top.

How about all the fabulous strategists that had 6000 Nasdaq targets and 1750 S&P 500 targets . . . in early 2000? These are not stupid people making these predictions. In fact, they are all a lot smarter than I am. They all graduated from MIT and Wharton. Where I am smarter is that I realize that unless I have next week's newspaper today, I can't predict next week. (That was a great "I Dream of Jeannie" episode. Roger Healy went right to the horse track with the newspaper.)

The methodology I have taught you is not about having opinions. It's not about predicting anything. It's not about trying to sound intelligent at a cocktail party. It's about the few simple correlations between price and volume action and massive moves in stocks which allow you to make money off of those moves. It's not always right. But it gives you the greatest edge out of all the thousands of trading systems and methodologies that I have researched, tested and traded over the years.

Rule #2: Control your losses. If your methodology is good, the profits should take care of themselves.

As I've mentioned, no investment methodology is perfect. While I am doing my best to help you become a winning investor, losses do happen. And you must deal with them by making sure they don't get out of control.

Always, always, always use a stop-loss once your buy order is executed. Typically, you should place your stop not more than

8% below your buy point. If you get stopped out, that's life. Just move on to the next opportunity . . . there will be many.

If your stock moves nicely in your favor, move your stops up as the stock is rising. How do I know all this? From my own mistakes.

In my own trading, what is almost as important as using stops is to simply watch your positions like a hawk. If you are long in a stock and see a sharp move down on heavy volume, that is a major red flag. When I see that, I don't wait for my stop to get hit. I am usually heading for the hills. Conversely, if you are short, and you see your stock move higher on heavy volume—again—don't wait for your stop to get hit. Just get out!

Rule #3: Isolate strong stocks when the market is weakest and isolate weak stocks when the market is strongest.

This is a very simple idea, but hardly anyone does it. When most everything in the market is getting trashed, look for the names that refuse to go down. There has to be a reason for it. Something good must be going on with those stocks. If the market resolves itself back to the upside, these are the names that will potentially become the strongest stocks very quickly.

When markets are ripping to the upside and you have a bunch of stocks that refuse to go up . . . what's going on there? There is obviously something wrong. And there may be opinions that say that they are solid companies, but we don't care what they think. We care what the market thinks. The market is the final arbiter. If the market decides to go down, guess what? Most likely, these stocks are going to be leading the plunge.

Rule #4: Become a student of market history.

One of the great turning points of my career was when I began digging through historical charts and asking myself questions like: "What did stock market tops and bottoms look like in the past?" and "What do all winning stocks throughout history have in common?" It sounds like a cliché, but it's true—history does repeat itself. The only caveat is that it never repeats itself exactly the same way. As you progress through the decades, you will find the same themes manifest repeatedly. But you have to be alert to the variations on those themes. Researching the past not only provides you with the criteria you need in order to identify new bull markets or the best stocks to be buying, but also helps you to maintain your objectivity. When you see what a severe bear market from the past looks like and the intensity of the fear that accompanies the final end of the bear market, then you will not get caught in the euphoria that inevitably occurs during the fake-out rallies that occur during present-day bear markets. The same holds true for major market tops.

Rule #5: Print out and tape charts of winning stocks to your refrigerator.

This is a corollary to Rule #4, but it deserves to have its own place in the sun. Nothing I've done has conditioned my brain to quickly and automatically identify winning stocks like seeing the profitable patterns from throughout history over and over again and then refreshing my memory on a regular basis. I'm being facetious about putting them on the 'fridge, but I am dead serious about making sure that you are surrounded with these examples so that your eyes will become heat-seeking missiles . . . constantly homing in on opportunities whenever you do your Nightly Preparation. It's not only essential for honing your brain's pattern-recognition ability, but also for keeping you in a rock solid discipline. You will avoid the temptation to make small but critical deviations from the winning models of the past—deviations that can make the difference between making or losing a lot of money.

Some traders I know post chart examples in their trading rooms. Others post them throughout their homes. And others stick them in binders and just make a point of reviewing the charts often. You figure out what's best for you.

Rule #6: Focus on what industry groups are doing.

I've said it before and I'll say it again. Minimum, 80% of picking a stock is making sure that it is in a sector that is going the right way. I am happiest when I am in a group that has been trading in a range for the last six months and pops out of that range to the upside on heavy volume. I'm going right to that group and asking which stocks are the leading stocks in the group and getting all over them.

From time to time as you eyeball charts in the evenings, you'll see a chart that has a picture-perfect breakout on heavy volume. Should you trade it? The only way for you to know is to first check to see if the sector or industry group that it's in is going up, because stocks move like schools of fish. It's not very often where some don't go along for the ride. Bottom line, you had better know if that group is in an uptrend above the moving averages with higher highs and higher lows and big volume on up days and lower volume on down days and all that other fun stuff. Of course, the opposite is true of stocks that you are looking to short.

Rule #7: Pay close attention to the New Highs list in order to stay on top of the leadership.

In Chapter 4, I showed you that healthy bull markets have strong leadership. Leadership is your strong core group of quality big-name stocks which are pushing continually to new 12-month highs, or that are in strong uptrends, trading within 10% of their 12-month highs. The way to find out whether that leadership exists is to constantly monitor the list of stocks that are making new highs, week after week. It's that simple. If you keep seeing the same big-name stocks that the analysts love to write about at the top of the list, then that's a positive for the rest of the market. If you see the leadership suddenly break down, however, it's potentially going to be meltdown time for the rest of the market. Is it possible to make money in a market that doesn't have leadership? Of course it is. I have been living this during the bear market we're in at the time of this writing. During a bear market, you're still going to be focused on breakouts, but during the inevitable fake-out rallies, the moves won't be as sustained and you'll be more of a trader than an investor. Plus, you'll also have major groups of stocks breaking down that you can short.

Rule #8: Listen to what people are saying, but don't do what they are doing.

I am a big believer in listening to the madding crowd—especially when they are tipping one way. When I see this happen during a bull market, I am seeing everybody make money far too easily. And finding the next hot stock becomes a topic of discussion in the supermarket line. The madding crowd will get it completely wrong again and again, so when you see this sort of thing happening, tighten your stops and get ready to retreat to the sidelines or go into shorting mode. Also, listen to what the analysts are saying. The same folks that led you astray in March 2000 will do it again, telling you to get out, right when the market is bottoming.

Rule #9: Evaluate yourself every month (just like a big company) and give yourself a grade.

I am a big believer in being brutally honest with myself about my trading performance. I look at what I did right and wrong and figure out ways to avoid making the same mistakes in the future. I suggest you do the same at least once a month, like I do. Don't just focus on the results, but look at the root causes and analyses that you did in order to trigger the action that you took. One good way to do this is to maintain a journal that documents every aspect of every single trade you make. Include the following:

- **Market analysis.** What was the market doing at the time and how did you interpret the indicators and sentiment?
- **Stock analysis.** In retrospect, how did the stock you trade meet or not meet your buying (or shorting criteria)?
- **Trade management.** Where did you enter the trade and why? How did you set your initial stop? What was the outcome when you exited?
- **Mental state.** What was your mental state at the time you took various actions? Did you place a trade on April 15 after having sent the IRS a huge check? Did you feel like you needed to get revenge somehow by making a fortune on a particular trade? Did that cloud your thinking?

Then, at the end of each month, look back at your journal and identify the mistakes you make. What was the cause? Was it lack of the right knowledge, or did you blow it because you did not exercise the proper discipline? What are you going to do in order to improve?

Countless studies have shown that the very act of monitoring performance tends to improve performance. But you have to get down to each step that contributes to your performance. Too many traders merely use the amount of money they make as the measurement of their performance. But that's like a manager on an assembly line measuring the performance of each of his workers by the amount of overtime they put in. You really have to measure the effectiveness of every critical decision you make in order to see improved returns in dollars and cents. So I heartily recommend getting into the nitty gritty as I've outlined above.

Rule #10: Learn how to profit from stocks that go down.

The happy times in the stock market are interrupted once in a while by periods of gloom. Yes . . . if you look back at history, the good times always return, but a lot of money always gets left on the table by traders who refuse to learn how to play the short side. I suggest that if you don't want to be sitting on the sidelines earning 2% interest from a money market fund during a bear market, reread Chapter 8 and learn how to short.

THE FINAL WORD FROM GARY

In this book, I have gone to great lengths to help you learn a complete methodology for successfully investing and trading in the stock market. Then, I have gone far beyond that by showing you what is necessary for you to successfully apply it. Some of what I am asking you to do is a bit out of the ordinary in that it involves looking at stock charts both on the weekends and on week nights.

But I only ask you to do this because I know that this discipline for success in the markets has worked extraordinarily well for me for years, as well as those I've taught it to.

And trust me, I wouldn't be doing it unless it was a lot of fun. Think of it:

> What is more thrilling than finding a stock that has the familiar look and profile of multitudes of winning stocks of the past . . . long base, breakout on heavy volume, a member of a hot industry group, favorable market conditions and so forth . . .
>
> Then . . . to watch that stock take off and keep going up, up, and away? *How much more entertaining is that than the hour of TV you might sacrifice each night to do your Nightly Preparation?*

In fact, I get such a kick out of seeing the results of my work, that it often overshadows the real down-to-earth reasons that I do what I do. I doubt that I have to remind you of them, i.e., financial security for your family, college education for your kids, a decent retirement, etc.

My sincere hope is that the knowledge I've shared with you will enable you to experience the same or better level of financial rewards and satisfaction that I have enjoyed over the years.

Best of luck,

Gary Kaltbaum

APPENDIX

Resources I Use

Even though I have many computer monitors at my office which display updated market information throughout the day, I do my most important research at home. I mention this because I want to convey that the tools I use are not esoteric or only available to Wall Street Institutions. *Anybody in the world can subscribe to these services.*

So now, here are the sources of information that I've referred to throughout this book:

Investors Business Daily

- For more information, go to www.investors.com or call 800-831-2525

Daily Graphs and Daily Graphs Online

- For more information, go to www.investors.com or call 800-472-7479

Investors Intelligence Weekly

- For more information, go to www.chartcraft.com or call 914-632-0422

TradingMarkets.com

- For more information, go to www.TradingMarkets.com or call 888-484-8220 x1

Improve Your Trading Results With Daily Setups From Gary Kaltbaum's Trading Services

On any given day, there can be dozens, even hundreds, of alluring setups for stocks to break out of a technical trading range. Most experienced traders know this and accept it, but there's a catch...

Only a few follow through to make big gains. Aren't these the ones you're interested in?

Now you can zero in -- instantly -- on these setups through Gary Kaltbaum's intraday and end-of-day alerts.

Gary Kaltbaum's ***"Intraday Setups Service"***
You will be notified intraday -- via e-mail during market hours -- of stocks with potential setups on an occurring basis. You will receive two or more alerts each trading day.

Gary Kaltbaum's ***"Setups I See For Tomorrow"***
You will be notified each evening -- via our private website -- of the stocks that have potential setups that Gary believes deserve his attention...and yours!

Gary's Service Will Provide His Personal Technical Analysis:

- Every breakout and consolidation setup you receive is screened by Gary for the same characteristics of stocks that have made homerun moves during bull and bear markets of the past.
- When Gary spots his Momentum Gaps, he will alert you. Gary's methodology identifies situations in which stocks have made moves in the direction of the gap.
- When Gary sees signs that the market may be making a real turn, he will notify you. Stay in sync with Gary's thoughts on intra- and end-of-day market timing indicators.
- Gary will offer his views on the leading industry groups and sectors so you can more effectively pinpoint your best opportunities for growth.
- You will be shown the kinds of information that have fueled the moves that capture headlines. No longer will you be thrown off balance by some of the noise in news media. Gary will cut through some of the B.S. and tell you what type of information he believes you can expect will affect stock prices.
- When corporate officers ("insiders") are reported buying or dumping their shares in massive amounts, Gary will give you warnings as he sees them so you can be ready if a potential surge or plunge materializes dead ahead.
- PLUS, you won't be alone. Gary will be there for you. You will have access to Gary's private message boards for subscribers only. Gary is sincerely motivated to help people pursue their trading goals and he will personally provide guidance on these boards. Of course, you could receive additional benefits through the group discussions.

How would you like to save many hours of having to looking through and analyze thousands of charts? PLUS, how would you like to take advantage of Gary's knowledge and let him tell you which stocks he sees with potential for having the Right Stuff on both the long and short side?

Sign up today for Gary Kaltbaum's "Intraday Setups" and "Setups I See For Tomorrow."
Call **1-888-484-8220 ext. 1,** or go to **www.GaryK.com** to begin your free trial now!

P.S. When you sign up for your free trial you will also receive Gary's FREE bonus reports.

PLUS RECEIVE 3 BONUS REPORTS FREE WHEN YOU SIGN UP FOR YOUR FREE TRIAL!

1. The Day's Most Powerful Trades–How To Anticipate When And Where They Will Occur Before The Market Opens
2. How To Analyze The Most Recent 15 Minutes Of Trading To Find Potential Explosive Moves
3. 7 Mistakes Daytraders Make And How To Avoid Them

Past Performance Is Not Indicative of Future Returns. All analyst commentary provided on TradingSubscriptions.com is provided for educational purposes only. The analysts and employees or affiliates of TradingSubscriptions.com may hold positions in the stocks or industries discussed here. This information is NOT a recommendation or solicitation to buy or sell any securities. Your use of this and all information contained on TradingSubscriptions.com is governed by the Terms and Conditions of Use and the Privacy Policy. Opinions expressed are our present opinions only. This material is based upon information that we consider reliable, but we do not represent that it is accurate or complete, and that it should be relied upon, as such.

ABOUT THE AUTHOR

Gary Kaltbaum is an investment advisor with over $125 million under management. For over 20 years, he has specialized in identifying and trading growth stocks in the intermediate-term time frame. He can be heard nightly on his nationally syndicated radio show, Investor's Edge. He runs a successful investment service that provides investors with timely alerts of opportunities occurring in today's markets. Gary is a FOX News Channel Business contributor and is regularly quoted by *The Wall Street Journal, Dow Jones News, Reuters, Associated Press, USA Today* and *Bloomberg.* For the latest information about Gary Kaltbaum, his investment service, TV appearances, and radio show, visit his website: www.GaryK.com.